Pushing Your Boundaries

The Feminine Principle in Business

Dear Wendy

Be the light and the love that you are

Pirj

Dr. Pirjo Friedman, D.D.S.

Edited by Shirrah Friedman and Miriam Sanua

PublishAmerica
Baltimore

First printing

ISBN: 1-4241-6334-X
PUBLISHED BY PUBLISHAMERICA, LLLP
www.publishamerica.com
Baltimore

Printed in the United States of America

Acknowledgments

My purpose in writing Pushing Your Boundaries *is to illustrate how working and sharing our knowledge with others can create a gateway for expanded potential and greater success. In this way, my team has been instrumental in creating, developing, and managing my successful business and enriching my life. Similarly, other individuals very dear to me have made significant contributions throughout the birth and development of this book, both directly and indirectly.*

My eldest daughter, Shirrah, has played an integral part in the making of this book. As the main editor, Shirrah contributed her expertise, innovative ideas, and many long hours, while busily pursuing her master's degree at the University of St. Andrews in Scotland.

Ken Burgin, the owner and creative director of Context Communications (www.contextcom.com), made a significant contribution during the preparation of this book. Ken, drawing from over 35 years of experience in the advertising and graphic communications industry, was responsible for designing the cover and doing the final edit.

Throughout the writing of this book, my youngest daughter, Tamar, has been continuously encouraging and supportive. Even my middle daughter, Kinneret, found time amidst her hectic final year at Queen's University, in Canada, to assist with insightful editing and final preparations of the book.

My heartfelt gratitude goes out to Daniela Topali and Evelyn Racelis. Daniela is a dedicated and loyal friend, and has done wonders keeping my mind at ease by running the clinic competently and effectively during my absence. Evelyn, too, has helped significantly in the clinic by adapting quickly and professionally following my retirement.

You have all played integral roles in the writing of this book, and it is as much yours as it is mine. Thank you for sharing my dream.

—Pirjo Friedman

Contents

Introduction

While my first book, Awakening the Entrepreneurial Spirit in You, Embracing Synchronicity, *was moving through the process of being published, I was in the process of formulating ideas relating to a different approach to my work. This entailed a change in how I saw myself—the focus now projected toward a new business scenario. At the same time, a whole new world was opening up for me—not through the outer environment but through the inner world of my dreamtime. I started to notice striking similarities between messages being conveyed by my higher self and events that were happening in the outer world. Clearly the key words in this new experience were an indication of the transformative process pushing me to move beyond anything I had ever known before. Words or phrases like: hidden key, elusive, reveal, transition, call to prayer, brought to life again, change and rebirth, deliverance from karma, foundation, balance and law of equilibrium are in fact keys to unlocking the deeper mysteries of life. They created a new moving picture that was unfolding right before my eyes. It was time to move from one existing frame of reference to a new one in terms of my life, attitudes, values, identity, and environment. No doubt the universe was throwing me these bones to keep me enthralled and intrigued as to my life's development.*

I have worked as a dentist for over 28 years in Finland, Israel, and now in Canada, running a successful practice with six associates in the Yorkville area of Toronto. Being fluent in four languages, I have taken the idea of diversity and evolved the concept into the microcosm of a community that expanded the business. My practice became a mini United Nations in its multi-lingual flair and diversity. This complemented and was congruent with my mission to create such an egalitarian environment. The book, Awakening the Entrepreneurial Spirit in You, *was an honest attempt at sharing my stories and experiences with you, the reader, about how I was able to evolve and create something out of nothing. These stories, nuances, experiences and little realizations along the way captured the essence of my success. My goal has been to inspire others to do the same in business and in their personal lives.*

Through the nature of my inquisitive and searching being, I permit myself to be open-minded to universal truths that have guided me through any doubts I might have experienced in the beginning. The universe in turn responded in its inimitable way by showing me that anything and everything is possible when you consciously let go of preconceived ideas and attachments and when you come from a place of trust. This is a feeling that resonates from deep inside. Messages become very clear. Like sign posts on a country lane pointing in many directions, they could lead you down any road, depending on where your intention lies. Through synchronistic events occurring in my life, I opened to reading the messages that were popping up at every turn, especially when decisions needed to be defined.

I made it my business to expand my expertise beyond what I considered mainstream education and awareness. Whether it was through the learning of the Silva Method of Mind Control, or Kung Fu, or the study of Kabbalah, meditation practices, hypnosis, or becoming a master Reiki Practitioner, it became clear to me that we are capable of pushing our boundaries. In fact there are no boundaries other than the ones that are self-created. It is my belief that each person's path may be different, but we all need to start somewhere. I have instilled this idea as a foundation for my three daughters who are out there in the world, independently exploring all their options—finding and learning to live their passion. In the same way, I have encouraged my staff to think outside of the box and grab the opportunities to move beyond their comfort level. Most have also had Reiki attunements and look to expanding their personal worlds into other areas of interest and focus. There is no doubt that this complement of skills and expanded awareness amongst my staff has made the environment what it is today. I branded the practice as "holistic" in the sense that it is not mainstream in its approach. The skills that my staff and I have acquired are incorporated into the practice. The best way to sum it up would be to say that coming into the practice is a wonderfully unique experience.

There are other aspects that have contributed to my success. I would attribute these to the connection that was established with the Women Entrepreneurs of Canada (WEC) organization. As mentioned in my previous book, networking was integral in establishing my business. Working relationships flourished at WEC. The buzzwords of the organization: support, champion, facilitate and promote, are clearly words that resonate from the feminine perspective and way of being. To this notion I will admit, I have openly subscribed, and in fact, it is the focus and mainstay of my work in the business arena in the future. Women are more open to sharing in this way, and through the years I came to understand the importance of "givers gain." The more I have shared, the more that I find has come back to me. I know that understanding and practicing this law of the universe has brought me much blessing. Teamwork is paramount in success—I realized a long time ago I could not be successful if not for the team I have built around myself. The results of our labors and endeavors speak for themselves. It is also my belief that we can take what we need from others' experiences and put the lessons to good use.

Building a new business is difficult for anyone, but I believe it is even more challenging for women. This is not because we are not as capable as our male counterparts or possess fewer or weaker entrepreneurial skills, but traditionally, our way of doing things has been foreign up until now in a world that has primarily run on masculine presumptions and attributes. Goals and aspirations in the business world may inherently be the same, but it is like looking at a coin; there are two very different pictures, one on either side, and yet there is only one value in representation. So the premise would be that in order for there to be a homeostasis of consciousness, there needs to be balance, both from the masculine and the feminine perspective, as to how and why we do what we do in the justification of the business fundamentals and ethics.

For the past few decades, women have been proving that it is possible to balance both a successful career and a thriving family life. How do we accomplish that? There is no shortage of self-help books listing what needs to be done in order to succeed and find happiness. The solution is for each of us is to experiment, find our own truth, and make that work for us. Something more significant is evolving at this present time and has been doing so for a number of years. In the same way that I found I could combine both the physical and spiritual elements that comprise my conscious reality, so this phenomenon seems to be sweeping the world. More and more women seem to be stepping up to the plate with a deeply honest and sincere desire to push for change in the world. One could say that in the beginning of the women's liberation movement and consciousness, competition with male counterparts became a battle of wills for control. Indeed, women were stepping into their masculine sides and operating on that basis to assert their rights. In more recent times, though, it seems that a great "softening" has taken place as we realize that the key is balance. We can be just as successful, if not more, operating from the feminine principles of sharing, due consideration, love, honor, respect, truth, humility, trust, creativity and openness. The reason for this is that the feminine attributes emulate those universal principles that essentially bring and sustain life. In fact these qualities are now being drawn from the conscious and unconscious pool of the psyche to manifest because the world is not in good shape. We have merrily danced our way down a garden path painted with glitter and "bling" as the younger generation refers to all that is glamorous and showy. We now realize this mentality of take, take, take is wreaking havoc on everything in life, spanning social, political, economical and environmental arenas. I am sure you agree; it is definitely time for change in consciousness. How do we transcend and make adjustments to the political, social, and economic upheavals that seem to be the order of the day, to a way of being that is far more equitable and balanced?

So far I have mentioned the word "experience" a number of times. The first was in describing my practice in its holistic environment. Anyone who has come into the practice and received a Reiki treatment, and who has had a discussion on universal principles or who has gone home with business cards and a referral for a specific type of professional help she has been seeking can attest to this "experience." In other words, their visit to this practice can be seen as a more encompassing experience and one that they would not necessarily find in other dental practices. Experience is also mentioned when referring to the process of moving beyond what, up to this point, has been a specific understanding you have had for yourself on how to start to push those parameters. The experience alters and becomes much broader once again. So whether all the outer world senses are evoked and stimulated, or an unconscious memory is struck or piqued through the "experiencing" of a business, this becomes a necessary ingredient for any successful and meaningful lasting relationship. In the practice itself, you find yourself working both sides, or components, of relationships—the spiritual and the physical. Communication has been an important solution with my office staff in undergoing the process of issue remediation. For this process I took a number of initiatives with the staff where the first was to give them the responsibility to solve any issues by themselves. If this did not work, then a further option would be mediation, whereupon perimeters have been established so situations don't end up triggering angry responses. I would use the team for this and had great results, not only face-to-face but also in sessions done from a distance. There have also been opportunities to work out past life issues amongst my staff.

In the working environment, the last resort in the process would be that one member leaves because you cannot work at it anymore, and there is resistance to healing the relationship. Today, the staff energy level in my practice is very good and stands as a testimonial to the mediation process and to communication in a team. This solution technology injects new options into the system. On the physical level, introducing advancements into the practice helps with confidence building and the expansion of staff skills. As an example, I introduced a successful Soft Tissue Management Program and oral cameras into the procedures of the practice to increase efficiency.

I have spoken about teamwork being paramount to success. Each step of the way you should also be familiar with your life, situation, and dreams. In my case, throughout my travails in the business world and my personal life, I valued and actively employed people whom I have had the pleasure to meet and form a relationship with, in order to move through any number of different experiences. The combinations of trades my dear friends ply span both the "spiritual" and "physical" realities of life. Each member of the team is highly specialized and skilled in his or her choice of life field. Not only have I realized that giving others opportunities to share their calling and passion through working together is useful in issue resolution, clarification, and in facilitation of healing, but that in this way we also contribute to the universal flow of energy and circuitry. There is so much growth and potential to be reached, not to mention we are each other's messengers in this combination of meaningful life dynamics. In the efforts you make to help yourself, by working with an individual or any number of partners, the mirror effect works as an indication for both recipients. And so, the dance of life intricately flows as we are continuously learning from each others' experiences. Interestingly, most of my friends, whom I call "my team," have, for the most part, moved away from work that specifically catered to the left-brain world. They shifted away from the masculine approach of structured logic and analytical work through some process—either a personal crisis or sudden deep realization—doing a one-hundred-and-eighty-degree turn to find something more fulfilling, sharing, and creative. It's as though they shifted focus from one hemisphere of the brain to the other. With the right brain being more creative and intuitive, the team is a group of individuals, each spiritual in her own unique way and incorporating both functions successfully, even though some may still be working or creating in corporate-style environments.

During the time I have worked with my team in guiding me through growing my dental business, I've found myself reaching a plateau. Something stirred inside of me wanting me to make a change. It was as if my heartstrings were now being pulled in another direction. This direction or path still had to reveal itself to me, but I knew it was time, and I was ready for it. It is almost as if by some divine contract, the universal computer reinstalled a new software program, or enhancement in order to re-calibrate the realm and function of this scenario. It set in motion the process of an alternate dimension of reality. Sessions with the team now focused on how to prepare myself and the practice, for a transition into this new scenario. I cannot emphasize enough the power this knowledge and the interactions have in bridging the gaps of our certainty, whether consciously or unconsciously, as we travel these unknown paths, one step at a time.

I began to carefully direct my energies to the consciousness of letting go. You can imagine that every aspect of who you have known yourself to be has to die a death. This is an essential process for something new to evolve. It feels like a carpet being ripped from under your feet as you take the leap from one identity to another. I found myself scrambling to reassemble a deep knowing of who I was before I became a dentist, albeit on the opposite scale of mainstream. What part of you is your true authentic self, you ask. How do you go about finding this out? Which direction do you move in? Who is there to support you through this process? Have you been in a situation where you are asking yourself these same questions? They may be questions focused more on your personal psychological death, but what about your business or your chosen profession? Some of us will deliberate and procrastinate for a period of time until we get over the fear of the unknown. Whatever the duration of time, we eventually get to the other side. Hopefully the transformation does not find us kicking and screaming, but rather flowing with the process in a graceful and easy a manner.

The formulation of a team around you is geared to support you through some of the key decisions you may have to make. Trust me—there will be a litany of those to deliberate on. Just operating out of that sharing mode makes a big difference in crossing the great divide between that which you are ready to let go of and the unknown. You must throw your arms open in blind faith. In following your deep, heart-felt aspirations in moving out into the world, you begin to experience yourself from a more creatively expressive dimension or perspective. There are a great many attributes that it may, if you have not embraced them before, be time for you to embody. You will notice that throughout the following chapters, where team members introduce themselves, who they are, how they came to do what they love and aspire to, their messages echo the themes that run through this book. These include being open to change. For this you would need to embody courage and fortitude to stay the course while you climb out of the confines of that which is known and comfortable to you and your structure. Daily routines and habits change, as well as your consciousness. It is no easy task to look at yourself in the mirror. Dedication and self-responsibility are key in pushing through when you are co-creating a new reality for yourself. Vision is another attribute creatively moving you to the next level to proactively create where you see yourself in the future. Embodying willpower and determination will assist you in moving through the transformation. It is important to make sure you pick yourself up from the hurdle when mistakes are made, and this is where the support of the team is so invaluable for reassurance and redirection. Finally, it is always a good thing to acknowledge what you have accomplished when all is said and done.

This book is a shared compendium of practical solutions, guides, road maps, and suggestions as to where to find support, particularly for women out in the business world or for those contemplating something new in their lives. I am particularly drawn within the parameters of my new business ventures, and accordingly, this book is for businesses transitioning from a structured environment to a more open, flexible and balanced one, in terms of the employer-employee relationship. This is a vital step in transformative processing—that the team will help businesses considering a transformation or for those with changes already underway and looking for further insight into the process.

In the Introduction of her book, The Female Advantage—Women's Ways of Leadership, *Sally Helgesen illustrates the kind of shift, pressure, and need for change that has already started to take place when she states, "By the late 1980s we had entered upon a period of unprecedented organizational upheaval, which, if anything, has intensified during the last few years. Organizations of every variety: business, educational, governmental, legal, medical, and religious were being pressed to explore new styles of leadership, new structures, new ways of motivating people, new ways of strengthening relationships of every kind." It is my mission to convey the interconnectedness between all of us. We work together in unity as a team in order to reach a new understanding of this relationship and begin to develop this consciousness as a process in our evolution as individuals, as well as collectively. "We do not work for, we work with," should be a new motto to be coined in the acceptance that we are all very much a valuable link in the global chain. Success is only success when it is shared amongst all. This is not meant to sound like a political statement—far from it. In fact, it is universal. The emphasis is to make the shift from the separation and division that has been the conscious and unconscious rift—the paradigm that employer and employee have created.*

The element of experience takes on a new paradigm as an enhancement of all our outer and inner senses while we learn more about ourselves. We come to the understanding as well, that we are to operate from all aspects of who we are. If we have a demanding schedule we need to look after the physical in order to stay fit in maintaining vital health. This abundance of health reflects our emotional, mental, and spiritual status, too. It is also imperative to look at the unconscious road maps, and this is why I have relied on the readings of an astrologer to be a guiding light in determining what my soul has asked for me to accomplish in this life, particularly the corrections I need and have chosen to make while doing what I love. Passion is the other light that cannot be ignored. We achieve much more and bring so much light, not only to ourselves but also to others around us, when we are involved in work or play that we are passionate about. Chances are we will have the greatest of success if this is the consciousness we keep in terms of our experiences and what we give as well as receive from our connections with others. Each of us is a link in a great chain that keeps the world operating and indeed flowing with the Grand Universal plan. The saying, "You are only as good as the weakest link," holds true for all of us. Everything we endeavor is about sharing with each other in order to support ourselves in becoming all we can be; that in fact, the chain is kept strong.

With a strong team around you, it is like an energy-balancing group, with each complementing the service and sharing of the other as they go out into the world for specific projects and work. Service is about helping people to reach the next step or level, to get to their goal in order to be successful, whatever it is they want to do or manifest in their life. Moving through this process for yourself and then for others, you advance from the logical energy of work and life and move through more and more and eventually into the creative energy. With a strong team, you become brilliant advocates for others in creating positive relationships all around you. The humanitarian qualities of your work manifest in your everyday approaches to the projects you are dealing with. It is also important to give yourself permission to have fun. Balance is key, as it is always good to give, to help, to heal; it is also good to nurture yourself. In other words, receive for yourself at least as much as you give out. In between all the busy-ness of life, remember that even with your team, you have the gift and opportunities of opening to greater unseen dynamics, such as enjoying silence together, increasing trust in your feelings, remaining centered even in the midst of chaos, and in childlike innocence enjoying the fantasy and passion of creating. The ultimate balancing act is attained in measure when we are open to new possibilities; when we are sharing, humble, yet dynamically creative and powerfully certain of who we are and what our service, love, or passion is in the world. We actively embody the feminine, along with masculine attributes, in a combined dance of creativity that will change how we see ourselves, how we see others, and how we see the world at large while being open to accepting ourselves, first and foremost, and then sharing this with all we meet for the betterment of mankind.

Apart from transcribing the tapes of the interviews with each of the team members; reformulating and editing the texts to a readable script, with the basis for the Introduction that Miriam and I collaborated on, I gave Miriam Sanua carte blanche to write the Introduction.

As an Holistic Integrative Coach and writer, Miriam combines her love and passion in sharing the heart as the gateway or Source of complete healing. Self-love as re-empowerment integrates the physiology, emotional, mental and spiritual aspects of being, consciously and energetically.

Miriam expressed her fascination in hearing, writing, editing and working with the blend and open scope of all the members of the team. Her understanding of the personal experiences, transformations and work and how each one's passion and service is so unique; divinely inspired as an expression of who they are, was both interesting to her and confirmation of the exciting times we live in. This illustrates the purpose behind transforming ourselves and transcending the consciousness of separation to one of truth and unity. It happens first and foremost on an individual level and then collectively.

Miriam inspires those she meets to jump out of the box, make a 180 degree turn in life and open to the awakening or remembering that we are pure love and spirit; here for the service of others and the world around us.

For more information about Miriam's work, she can be contacted at mirisan@sympatico.ca.

—Pirjo Friedman

Marcelene Anderson—
Strategic Management Consultant

Photo: Yanka Van der Kolk

Marcelene and I first met through the Women Entrepreneurs of Canada organization (WEC) several years ago. During my presidency at WEC, Marcelene helped bring the organization back to its feet by facilitating strategic planning sessions with the board. Although the process was long, involving more than 20 hours of work, it was useful in reinstalling some much-needed inspiration and direction within the organization. During this collaboration, I learned that Marcelene was a wonderfully bright and refined lady of integrity who possesses an impressive array of skills and talents.

When I decided to sell my dental practice, I knew I wanted to create a new business venture, although I was uncertain what sort of business I wanted to create. There were many things I wanted to do, and what I needed was to clarify my thoughts and outline my ideal business idea. Even once I had established the nature and goals of my new business, I still required help in illuminating my approach and strategies, since this business incorporated an entirely new concept of motivational networking and entrepreneurial practices, both for the world and me. Watching Marcelene do her magic at WEC, I knew that she was the one to help me through this process. Our discussions revolved around the concept of the new business, Motivational Networks, and incorporated the ideas and philosophies I believe in, and that I wished to convey as a platform for my business. Furthermore, we discussed the type of clientele I would be targeting in my new business: individuals who have been in business for a while and who have undergone a change of heart, feeling the urge to transform both personally and professionally. Perhaps they feel that they have had enough of their old life and wish to pursue a new career encompassing their passions and interests. Or perhaps they have not found fulfillment but are out there, actively seeking it.

Aside from clarifying and defining my business concept and strategies, Marcelene and I focused on ensuring a smooth transition from my present business to my future business for my employees and myself. We did this by forming a clear vision of the end result that would be in place, and of the shift that will have taken place, using a thinking-backwards approach to the future process. Forming and holding a clear picture of the desired outcome is one of the vital ingredients to success—if we can't see it, it is unlikely that we can create it.

Marcelene's expertise and insight have been invaluable in the process of creating my new business. Today, as the company begins to materialize, I realize that the essence of Motivational Networks is much like the process of its creation—it is about the team, being guided through the steps, and having reassurance that you are not alone in the process. The team is there to hold your hand and support you.

—Pirjo Friedman

The essence of my work is developing strategic plans with individuals and companies. In my business, Raven Strategic Consulting, I specialize in strategic management, which involves a combination of plan formation, successful implementation of the plan and related changes, and the maintenance of high performance over time as to achieve the desired results. I am the founder and president of Raven Strategic Consulting and also an associate of the Centre for Strategic Management International, an affiliation of master facilitators based in 38 centers and 20 countries. Over the past 24 years, I have also gained experience and expertise in change management, leadership development, and performance management.

Strategic management assists individuals and businesses in envisioning their desired future and in planning for where they want to be. The purpose of the strategic plan is to develop a set of measures, sometimes referred to as goals, to assess whether they have achieved their desired future. Additionally, the plan includes an assessment of the internal and external factors that may represent the strengths, weaknesses, opportunities, or threats that could influence the company's strategy. Essentially, the plan is a bridge from where the business is today to where you intend it to be at a certain point in the future. This bridge includes a set of core strategies selected as to close the gap between the vision of the future and the present reality and is aimed at achieving the targeted results.

There are numerous approaches to developing a strategic plan, and I have studied and applied half a dozen of them in my work. One of the most helpful approaches is the Systems Thinking Approach™. Its basis is to think backwards from the future one aspires to, to the changes one should implement in the present to create it. Although this approach is very common in many parts of the world, it is less common in North America, where analytical or linear approaches to planning and problem solving are the norm. In my experience, the complexity of businesses and organizations today demands a systems-wide perspective in order to plan for the future, to solve today's problems and dilemmas, and to accommodate the introduction of new systems, practices, programs, and products aimed at serving the ever-changing needs of customers.

The initial step in creating a strategic plan is to crystallize the individual's or company's vision of where they would like to see themselves in the future and to formulate a mission statement reflecting their purpose as an organization. During this stage I ask my clients to take a step back, examine the bigger picture, and ask themselves: What is our mission as a company? What is my reason for being? I ask them to imagine the ideal future they would like to experience within the next five to ten years. For those that find it difficult to envision their future goals, I recommend pretending that they are living five or ten years from now, and ask them to tell me the story of their lives in the past few years. Alternatively, they can imagine that they are watching a movie of their ideal life several years from now. What does the movie reveal? What has made them successful? How was their company different from others in the industry? What milestones did they need to pass in the process? During my discussions with Pirjo, for example, we established that being an entrepreneur, her professional and personal missions are interrelated. The ultimate purpose in her personal life is to help and advise women in choosing their own path—to guide and support them in their search for meaningfulness in their lives. Pirjo's vision for her new business, Motivational Networks, is to share information, wisdom, and insight in guiding people who proactively change themselves, and thus helping their businesses become healthy and successful.

A key component of defining the future is to consider the core values by which an individual or a group intends to function, collaborate, and treat their clients. Core values reflect the shared core beliefs. Outlining the core values is particularly important for companies, as building a business based on values and thereby providing excellent service to customers can become a key competitive strategy and differentiator from other similar businesses. In my opinion, Pirjo's practice is more value-focused than most other businesses. Her values have contributed to the success of her dental clinic in the past, and also stand as the basis of her future business. Some of these values include: practicing the "Givers Gain" approach by balancing giving and receiving in all aspects of work and life; respecting and celebrating diversity by recognizing others' capabilities and utilizing their knowledge and skills; enhancing team work by recognizing and appreciating each individual's contribution, committing to talent development by investing in others' continuous education and expansion of skills and wealth; sharing leadership by distribution of information, power and responsibility; supporting and augmenting personal fulfillment by encouraging personal responsibility for self and the pursuit of one's life purpose; making the clients the number-one priority and treating them as more than just the next dollar in the till; and the integrating of body, mind and spirit.

Once the vision, mission, and value statements have been formulated, the company's measures of success, or what might be more commonly referred to as long-term goals and objectives are outlined. It is important to keep in mind that these measures of success or goals should be clear, measurable, include a time frame, and most importantly, be realistic. Pirjo has outlined the following goals for her new business, for accomplishment in a five-year time period: to create wealth and abundance for the business and its employees; to build a replicable business model exemplifying new principles of cooperation, wealth co-creation and customer service; to establish a workplace where employees are fully engaged and take responsibility for their careers and personal fulfillment; and to advise businesses and women in particular, showing them a new and different way of working and succeeding.

Outlining the company's vision and goals is important since we often get caught up in the present and engaged in the day-to-day details, causing us to lose sight of our ultimate goals. This is a natural human tendency, which can be avoided by clearly stating our vision and goals in our strategic plan. Defining our goals and objectives is worthless, however, if we do not have a way of measuring whether or not we have achieved them. Measures of success should therefore cover all aspects of the business, such as, employee satisfaction, customer satisfaction, financial viability and stakeholder satisfaction. Each may include various methods of measuring the success of the company, and choosing the relevant measures should be based on the nature of the business, the practices employed, and the goals and objectives stated. Financial success, for example, can be measured by gross revenue, profitability, stock price or shareholder value to indicate if the strategies employed are achieving the financial bottom line. Stakeholder satisfaction refers to any person or organization that has an impact on or is affected by the company. Stakeholders may be shareholders, suppliers, customers, companies that provide a service, such as banks or accounting firms, networks the company is involved in, the government or the community in which the company operates as a whole. With regard to employee satisfaction, we may look at retention of employees, how many new applicants the company is attracting, or the number of alumnae in the company's employee club. Customer satisfaction can be measured by percentages of customer retention, repeat business and referrals, as well as other measures that can be derived from methods such as customer-satisfaction surveys.

The next step in creating the strategic plan involves identifying both internal and external influences and issues that are likely to affect the company's strategy. Internal factors to be assessed include such things as an analysis of the organization's finances, its core values, business design, leadership capability, human resource management, rewards for performance, cross functional teamwork, technology, and its core competencies. Influences external to the organization may impact it by presenting threats and opportunities. When analyzing the external environment of the company, it is useful to scan factors such as socio-demographics trends, competition, political forces, technological advances, economic developments, and legal issues. One should try to predict how these factors are likely to change in the future, and how they may affect the company. Typical questions to ask may be: What are the social demographics likely to be in the next five years? Who will be the competition? How could the economy evolve? What may be the key political factors? What impact would technology have on the company's operations? Analyzing these environmental influences is an important tool in the formulation of strategy and in strategy development, as it is useful in identifying potential threats and opportunities for the company. Analyzing these internal and external forces is essential for matching the company's resources and capabilities to the competitive environment in which it operates.

Once we have established what we strive to accomplish in the future, an analysis of the gap between our desired future and our present standpoint is required. A thorough assessment of this gap will indicate what steps and actions, or core strategies we will need to take in the future in order to close the gap, considering our weaknesses, building on our strengths, minimizing the threats, and capitalizing on potential opportunities. Typically, core strategies will deal with aspects of the business such as growth, productivity, innovation, human resource management, and leadership.

The process of closing the gap between a company's current situation and its goals will require a transition period and an operational plan. In order to ensure a smooth evolution, a coherent transition plan is needed. The plan is particularly important in order to keep all employees on the same wavelength, ensuring that their spirit does not collapse due to unnecessary confusion and anxiety of an unknown future. In Pirjo's dental office, for example, her team is very efficient and independent in their current positions and roles. With the prospect of selling the practice looming in the air, however, her staff is unavoidably struggling with new concerns—who will be the new owner of the practice? Will they continue to be employed under the new ownership or will they be replaced? Even if they will continue to work in the practice, would the atmosphere remain the same? Will they continue to enjoy working there? One of the key elements of the transition plan is maintaining candid and compassionate communication with colleagues and employees. It is recommended that the communication between employers and their team be an informal, two-way communication channel, and that the team will be consulted in the visualization of the future and the personalization of the transition stage.

A strategic plan is not set in stone; it is a dynamic, cyclical process. As people and businesses grow and evolve they should continuously ask themselves whether there are any new opportunities or ideas that can take their business and life to the next level, or whether new weaknesses and threats have emerged which could jeopardize their success. Over time, new gaps between the desired and reality may come to light, along with new strategies to close them. Therefore, the strategic plan should be revisited on an annual basis and updated with any new information.

Strategic planning requires a great deal of personal reflection, honestly evaluating past accomplishments, learning from past experiences, and applying them to any future processes. Formulating and clarifying your vision and goals based on personal reflection provides you with the opportunity to superimpose your values, enthusiasm, and talent. The greatness of who you are gradually unfolds as you peel away the layers of self-limiting beliefs and concerns into an empowering belief system, integrating the physical, emotional, mental, and spiritual constructs of who we want to be in our growth towards greater self-awareness.

—Marcelene Anderson

You can learn more about Marcelene Anderson at: www.ravenstrategic.com

Kerry Barnes—Personal Trainer

Photo: Yanka Van der Kolk

Kerry and I met through a mutual friend. When I first started training with him, we did it in my home, using door frames, furniture, stairs, walls, yoga balls, the floor...anything, really. Though this worked well for us, when I moved to my present apartment building where there is a well-equipped gym, the sessions became even more enjoyable and effective.

Training has made me feel significantly better about myself. I look better and feel firmer, fitter, and more energized. I find that working out is especially crucial during stressful times. No matter what pressures I am facing in my life, having a session with Kerry takes me out of that frame of mind entirely. A workout energizes my body, drains away the stress, and leaves me feeling relaxed and satisfied.

Today I have an ingrained need to exercise. I think everybody does, especially after they become used to working out. Once you get into the habit of exercising, it becomes something you want to do more than something you need to do. You just know you will feel so much better afterwards. Sometimes it is difficult to drop everything in the middle of the day for the workout, but once you prioritize your exercise, you just do it, scheduling everything around it. Unless I am traveling, I never cancel Kerry, and he never cancels me!

After a period of regular exercising, I not only feel healthier, but I also experience significantly less pain. Being a dentist for 30 years has involved sitting in an awkward position for long periods of time, placing immense strain on my lower back, neck, and wrists. The pain inherent in my line of work has been alleviated through regular and proper training. Kerry has also enhanced my awareness of which muscles I am working. When I carry things, for example, I am now conscious of which muscles should be working, thus avoiding injury to my back and other weak areas.

Kerry is not only a great trainer but he is an amazing source of knowledge on any subject. He is always extremely generous with his know-how on nutrition and correct exercising, demonstrating how to maximize the positive effects and minimize health risks. Our workouts are always accompanied by interesting discussions, and I often consult with him on other topics. Most importantly, Kerry has a great sense of humor. We work out while joking around, which makes our sessions very enjoyable.

—Pirjo Friedman

Born and raised in Toronto, I decided at age 17 to travel before starting university. I ended up living in California for ten years! I attended California State University as a pre-med studying biochemistry, and subsequently worked in the nursing field for several years. When I returned to Toronto, I looked for my "spot" in the Canadian medical landscape—I sought a career that would stimulate and invigorate me. An acquaintance that was aware of my fitness and medical background referred me to the Adelaide Club, a large fitness facility in downtown Toronto. I spent nearly ten years working for that club, beginning in 1990, and that's where I started my training career. I believe that all the situations you find yourself in and all the choices that you make in your life are always indicative of "being in the best place for you to be." Being a trainer has worked out well for me. Although I could have been anything: a doctor, a nurse or an actor—I most enjoy the flexibility that my profession affords me, the flexibility of being an entrepreneur.

When I first returned to Canada, the concept of "personal training" did not exist in this country. In fact, I was considered to be in the vanguard of the personal training industry in Canada. During the early 1990s, five colleagues from competing facilities and I decided that the services offered by each of our facilities were not sufficient to be considered "professional" training. During those early years, high-end fitness facilities employed university-educated, highly accredited fitness consultants. These consultants worked for a fixed salary, providing advice to club members. Since these services were included in the membership fees, they did not present a profit center for the clubs, in contrast with other services like massage and physiotherapy. As a result, fitness clubs did not invest in high salaries for the fitness consultants, and since the latter did not have an opportunity to increase their yearly pay, many consultants were unmotivated and bored. It was from this seed that we started the personal training industry.

We started by establishing personal training accreditation programs, collaboratively, within each of our high-end fitness clubs, as we all were directors of our individual club's fitness programs. Our clubs targeted individuals that had a good grasp of physiology, anatomy, nutrition, and other requisite qualifications we deemed necessary for becoming a trainer. However, since there was no model available on how to develop a personal training business, I specifically offered the fitness team members at the Adelaide Club the opportunity to waive their fixed salary, and in return the Adelaide Club would allow them to build their businesses within the Club facilities for a period of 90 days.

At first I was the only one to pursue this option. Not surprisingly, it was difficult to convince other salaried consultants to give up their guaranteed paychecks without proof that this new concept of mine would work! But I believed in my vision. During the three months that the club carried me, I proceeded to find people who were willing to pay me out of their own pocket for information similar to that given by the club's salaried consultants. What I could offer that was unique, however, was time. In 1992, the Adelaide Club had almost four thousand members; it was technically impossible to offer them all daily or even weekly consultations. Members would end up receiving individual appointments only once every few months, if they asked for it, or would try to "catch" the consultants with a quick question while they were walking through the gym. In contrast, the personal trainers working at the clubs, like myself, had nothing but time, and as a result could offer members exclusive daily training sessions. At first I offered many complementary sessions, but as time went by and I accumulated a group of regular clients, I reduced the complementary sessions and increased my hourly rate. After three months I started to get the attention of the club and other consultants.

They began realizing that while they were working 8-hour days, earning $12 an hour; I was working three hours a day or less, and earning more! During the first three months, after I had waived my salary at the club, I kept 100% of my earnings. Once the 90 days were over, however, the club wanted in. We agreed that out of every $100 I earned I would give the club $20. With this agreement, even when I was charging $25, I would work four appointments in the day and earn $80: the equivalent of seven working hours.

During this time, although I was working only few hours a day, I was busy networking and developing my business. I was also meeting with other fitness clubs to ensure that their training certification programs were all developing concomitantly. Once the guidelines of the program were defined and coordinated, our group shifted the focus outside the fitness industry to universities and high schools. Our goal was to offer an exciting new avenue for students and working professionals who were looking for a positive career path change, challenging them to develop their own businesses while at the same time contributing to the professional growth of our new industry. It has worked out to be bigger than anything the original five could have dreamed of! Until 1993, if you graduated from university with a physical education degree you became a gym teacher or coached high school and university teams. Alternatively, you could work in government fitness, or find work with an equipment manufacturer. It was not until 1992, when Susan Lee and colleagues established the Canadian Personal Trainers Network (CPTN), that guidelines and requirements were set for a national accreditation specific to personal training. CPTN has helped set the Canadian professional standard that exists today.

One of the main developments the industry has achieved relates to the public's acceptance of the personal training profession. Today we no longer have to convince clients of the value of working with a trainer as an adjunct to a normal fitness routine. It is very common these days for a person to meet with a personal trainer weekly for nutritional advice and program structuring. But this was not always the case. A little over a decade ago, if I mentioned that I was a personal trainer, a common reaction would have been "You're a what?" Although the profession had been developing in California for over a decade by then, in Canada the concept that people would pay for a trainer was foreign. The reactions were similar to those massage therapists had to deal with a few decades ago, when people would equate those professionals with a practice that was, well, questionable. We have come a long way!

What is interesting about training the physical body is that people are more alike than one might perceive. Individuals' bodies have many commonalities, resulting in similarities in training structures in a diverse client profile: professional athletes, rehabilitating burn victims, seniors, plain old moms and dads. Another similar characteristic between all human beings is their need for movement and exercise. Some people are naturally more active than others, but I guarantee that if all you do is sit behind a desk, eat and drink, at some point your body will break down. It may be at the age of 30, 50 or 70, but it will happen. Exercising is beneficial for dietary purposes as well, since the more you exercise, the more active muscle you grow, and that means you get to eat more! Muscle accounts for higher rates of metabolism, resulting in a faster, more efficient burning of calories. This explains why men, who are naturally more muscular than women, can eat significantly more and not gain as much, if any, weight. Since women lack this added muscle bulk, they must compensate by eating less or being considerably more active.

I estimate that throughout a typical busy day in the corporate world, one taps into roughly 20% of their physical potential. Utilizing the remaining 80% is vital, since if you don't, you'll lose it! And once this is gone, individuals become prone to disease, heart attacks, and arteriosclerosis. This fact is well known today. In my experience, however, I have noticed that unless these risks become a reality, it continues to be under prioritized.

Working as a trainer with numerous clients over the years, I have come across all possible excuses used by people to rationalize their lack of exercise. The most common complaint voiced by professionals is lack of time. Throughout my career I have worked with some of the busiest people in the city: actors, law partners, corporate executives, and entrepreneurs. Despite the extreme levels of responsibility and stress in some workplaces, however, I claim that everybody has the time—nobody is *that* busy. Even if you happen to be the busiest person in the city, if you experienced a heart attack today, your priorities *would* change and you *would* find the time to exercise tomorrow, by understanding that not doing so may be fatal. Regardless of what exercise you choose to use, and whether you are training individually or with a trainer, issues of time will be minimized if the training receives the priority it deserves.

Another commonly voiced concern relates to fatigue: "I am already so tired; I do so much in the day that I couldn't possibly do more. I would just be wiped out!" While this may sound familiar, it could not be further from the truth. In fact, incorporating a modicum of suitable physical activity, especially in the morning, will create an available pool of energy to carry you through the day, as well as speed up your metabolism. Pirjo, for example, leads a very busy life, juggling the management of her dental clinic, her new writing career, and other future plans. Despite her busy schedule, however, by maintaining a regular workout routine at least twice a week in the mornings, she feels more energized and vibrant than ever.

All exercise and training routines should be tailored to each individual's goals and objectives. Following a strenuous training routine may seem difficult and therefore worthwhile, but if it is not focused on your particular needs, you may be simply treading water. The results do not always have to lean towards the aesthetic, for instance, but could point in other directions as well—an increased energy level, for example. The functionalities that you are addressing in your workout need to be clearly defined. When Pirjo first started working out with me, the components of her training structure were focused on her functional capacity. As a dentist, Pirjo had a lot of wrist flexion and extension, resulting in carpal issues and wrist pain. These problems were alleviated by appropriate strengthening exercises and stretches, while incorporating ideas of rest and appropriate icing throughout her workday. Together, we worked on building strength across her shoulders. After a year of focusing on her functional capacity, Pirjo became stronger and less restricted by the work-related pain, and we eventually shifted the focus to her abilities and needs as an individual, not as a dentist.

So far I have discussed the importance of *output*—the physical activities that burn calories. Incorporating *input* in your training—the nutritional component—is just as important, if not more so. While you may burn 400 calories in forty-five minutes of output, it's possible to eat it all back in less than two minutes! Some of this intake, such as protein, carbohydrates, and fiber, may be used by the body, but the remaining calories, regardless of whether they are derived from protein, carbohydrate or fat, will be stored as fat. Forever! Excess input can therefore cause significantly more damage than any output can offset.

As a certified trainer, I am qualified and experienced to provide nutritional advice to my clients. But my knowledge has its limits. Great trainers have extensive professional networks with other specialized care providers (registered dieticians, massage therapists, physiotherapists, sports medicine specialists, etc.) to support what they know. This professional support becomes an invaluable tool when training individuals with various metabolic and physical conditions: diabetes, Chrone's sufferers, amputees, and others who require careful, intensive, nutritional and program guidance. Nutritional advice often includes diet structuring—what and how much people should eat. In order to adhere to this structure, individuals should be educated about nutrition, learning exactly what it is that they are eating, what is the appropriate amount of protein they need to consume, and so forth. This is particularly important in our society, since the North American society is typically plagued by over consumption.

Generally speaking, all diets work...in the short term! The secret is in the structuring. Following any diet structure in the short term will show results since the body is forced to change and adapt. Once adaptation is reached, however, the body reaches stasis, and will not change any more. You *could* prolong the change to your body by continuously switching diets, for example, following Montignac for four weeks; switching to South Beach, then Atkins and so forth. But this is impractical, to say the least! Adherence to a diet structure is the main challenge for most people following weight-reduction or aesthetic protocols. Overall program success is achieved only when concurrent change is maintained in areas *other* than diet; exercise, eating pattern, rest, and so forth. Also, most people have difficulties adhering to certain types of diet structures due to unrelated factors, such as lack of time to cook or social and professional engagements, which require dining out frequently. It's hard to ask for an "Atkins" (protein only) meal when dining with clients at a Mexican restaurant!

Another consideration that needs to be taken into account when structuring a successful diet and exercise program is behavior modification. Many diets lack this element, and therefore prove inefficient in the long run. For example, many people spend thousands of dollars at various fat farms, fit farms, boot camps, and other weight loss programs. While these programs direct the individual to consume precise, calorie-calculated meals and perform physical activities, which will inevitably lead to weight loss throughout the duration of the program, they do not modify one's behavior. Once the individual returns home, to reality, cooking his or her own meals, eating out, and munching at work, the weight is likely to return. Without the reasoning of how, when, and why we eat, we can't possibly know when we are making the mistakes that doom us to diet failure!

An important detail about diets, one that is hardest to convince clients of, is the fact that a person needs to eat in order to lose weight. One of the main misconceptions regarding dieting is that if you want to lose weight you must eat less, restricting intake while maximizing output. What people may not realize is that if your body requires 1200 calories a day to exist and you burn 800 more calories exercising, make sure you consume 1600 to 1800 calories that day. The output is necessary in order to manipulate bodily changes. If you output more than you intake, you may be seeing results in the short term, but since no raw material is being consumed, you are neither building muscle nor propagating the "feeding" of the system, leading to eventual mechanical system breakdown. Adhering to a diet that supplies your body with everything it needs is crucial. Supplementation is often vital when this cannot be achieved naturally. For example, if your goal is building muscle, you must intake enough protein. This is often unachievable, since chewing through enough chicken per day to reach the required protein levels may be difficult for some people. Supplementation through vitamins and whey protein for example, is an easy solution in this case.

Exclusion-based diets do not work, mostly due to emotional aspects. For example, if I were to tell a smoker they could never have another cigarette, chances are they will not be able to quit. The thought takes away their desire to quit. On the other hand, if I give them one cigarette in a glass case, and allow them the choice to break the glass if they really need to smoke, psychologically this relieves the need, since they know the option is there. Dieting is not much different. If you deny yourself a certain food, or restrict your calorie intake drastically (less than 1200 calories for an active day), I guarantee you will not be able to adhere to the diet. All it takes is one 'bad moment' for your cravings to take over your diet structure. As opposed to normal, healthy hunger which allows you to eat foods that satisfy your body's nutritional requirements, when you deprive your body of its fuel, your hormonal hunger cravings will lead you to consume sugary and high fat foods, none of which satisfy your physiological needs.

The most effective method of controlling and adhering to your diet is by logging both your output and particularly, your input. I can be there for your physical training, but I cannot be there to watch what you put in your mouth the other 23 hours of the day! Controlling your nutritional component should be entirely up to you. However, even if you do not adhere to your programming one hundred percent, don't punish yourself. A healthy and realistic nutritional structure will allow you to have treats. For example, if you go to a wedding and indulge, your body will not be able to process all that food and will therefore dispose of it. The one-time event will not cause any damage. However, if you were to go on a cruise and eat that way for a week you will gain weight since your body cannot manipulate the excesses and excrete them fast enough. Instead, your body will store the excesses.

Another important element of success in your training and nutritional programming is having good support networks. Sometimes, for example, some husbands and wives don't want their spouses to look better. They are intimidated; afraid that they will be left behind as the confidence and self-image of their spouse increases. Husbands will subconsciously sabotage their wives' progress, for instance, by bringing them flowers and chocolate as a reward for their hard work. Being in a troubled relationship will affect not only the control of your programming, but also your physicality, as you become tired and agitated from the psychological stress emerging from such issues. Your physical, aesthetic, and performance development will be inhibited, and you will not get anywhere until you deal with these issues. Pirjo is an example of this situation. Despite how much she wanted her previous relationship to work, it did not. All the energy she put into improving the relationship was in vain and therefore wasted, building up frustration, disappointment, and anger. Once she understood this, ended the relationship and resolved to let go of her issues, her progress and success increased significantly. In my perspective as a trainer and physiologist, Pirjo has improved significantly in the last few months. She is stronger and more energized, which enables her to be more active in her life. She is enjoying training more from a physical, emotional, and mental perspective, particularly since she is seeing the results. She is looking good, the weight is peeling off, and she is happy since she is staying the course and reaching her goals.

North Americans are attracted to quick fixes like: a cream, a pill, or pieces of equipment that will help them reach their goals instantly. If people exercised and followed realistic nutritional programming, they would succeed; but when they hear it may take several months, many are no longer interested. They want it *now*, and thus provide opportunities for the billion-dollar diet and fitness industries. These industries are based on the predication that you are going to try, you are going to fail, and that you will try again. And again. And again. If the quick fixes really worked, they would all go out of business! Commercials on television guarantee flat stomachs and defined abs simply by using a certain machine, pill, or shake. It all looks very promising, but it absolutely doesn't work. The industry uses many tricks to lure you in. For example, remember the guy in the commercial that transforms his overweight body into a defined, lean, muscular body in 90 days, over four pictures? Sure, the pictures *are* real, not doctored. What they do not reveal, however, is that the model was lean and muscular to begin with, and was paid to reverse the procedure. The company paid him to gain sixty pounds of fat, and then tracked his progress as he trained back down to his normal weight and physique!

Great trainers educate people. They empower them. They give them the knowledge and confidence and self-esteem to elevate themselves to an increased state of well-being. Our clients trust us to share their innermost secrets and insecurities of who they are and what they really want. I have always felt a powerful, emotional connection to everybody I have worked with because of this. And that is why I wouldn't be doing anything else!

—*Kerry Barnes*

You can learn more about Kerry Barnes at: www.kerrybarnes.com

Olina Budin—Healer

Photo: Yanka Van der Kolk

It appears that the paths of those with similar outlooks toward life will eventually meet. Olina first came to my dental practice, attracted by our offer of Reiki treatments and seeking similar minded professionals to care for her oral health.

Although we became friends from the start, I did not fully realize all that Olina did as a healer. It was not until I invited her to give a presentation to the office staff that she revealed her experiences with lymphatic therapy, chakra balancing, and aromatherapy. Following the presentation I made an appointment to see her. I was very satisfied with the treatment—I was in seventh heaven! Healing happens in stillness and relaxation, and these feed back to one another, particularly if you have constant stress, which is detrimental to your health. The treatment was effective in getting me to that relaxed state. Since then, I often share my experiences with others, enthusiastically promoting Olina's work and abilities.

In my opinion, one of the most important messages in Olina's story is the importance of tuning in to the guidance of one's inner voice and moving ahead in life with what suits you. We all experience various health challenges throughout our lives. Some of us are open to noticing these issues as awakenings, but not everyone wants to listen. While some of us decide to change our ways, others may resist and simply push forward with whatever is coming to them. If we keep doing the same thing year in and year out, physically, emotionally and mentally, the consequences will catch up with us. But if we choose to be diligent and responsible, doing everything we can to maintain optimal health through a preventative approach, these consequences may be averted. Change does not happen if we do not solve the issues in one way or another.

Olina's story emphasizes the importance of being proactive, rather than dragging along until we have no choice. One must get out of the "wounded victim" consciousness, before becoming a prisoner of that mind set. As you begin to heal the physical, emotional, and mental aspects of your life, other areas also come into alignment with this expanded awareness of the self, expressed as increased creativity and success in achieving your goals.

—Pirjo Friedman

My experience with healing began in childhood. I grew up with a family that had rarely gone to see a doctor. Whenever one of us four children was sick in any way, my father would go out and pick herbs to treat us—it was his hobby. My father was the first to show me that the administration of herbs and the application of home remedies passed on from generation to generation were powerful conduits for bringing our bodies into a state of harmony with nature. My father had even healed his tuberculosis by applying a combination of traditional medicine and the idea that willpower is the inner healer. For many years, however, I took my father's knowledge for granted. It was not until I went back to school to study herbology that I realized *my father knew all of this!*

My mother contributed to my experience with healing by being a spiritual person. Although we were Catholic, I recognize today that my mother's faith had nothing to do with religion, but rather, she was living every day the way that I am living now. My mother lived her life as the embodiment of Spirit that connects us all through unconditional love. She had the gift of feeling and of being one with that Spirit, and she used her gift to uplift everyone she met. Everyone, including my three children, loved to be in her presence. My mother was a simple country woman, but she was gifted. She was not simple-minded, but simple in her child-like innocence of being able to trust and to have faith in God. She had the ability to communicate with God through the presence of everyday virtues such as courage, patience, and the embrace of change as part of life; recognizing the unlimited strength and power that we all possess and are a part of; having God experience Himself through us the way He meant for us to experience Him in our everyday lives; teaching us to accept what life brings; and making our learning more powerful, and yet more humble.

I count my blessings to have had such teachers in my life.

Our lives are characterized by continuous change, and rather than fearing it, I welcome it. Letting go of fear entails letting go of our ego. Not that the ego is a bad thing—on the contrary, it protects us; but it is based on fear, which restrains us. I am able to let go of my fear by putting my trust in God. I realize more and more these days that I am God's servant, and this is the reason I live my life. Up until this point in time I ran a holistic center in Toronto. These days, however, I am amidst another stage of change in my life—a new chapter of helping others in a more profound way.

When I first started working I was a hairstylist. I loved it, since it allowed me to be creative and work with people—two things I enjoy. At the time, I did not realize that I was working with the "Sahasrarachakra"—the crown chakra, also known as "the gateway to the higher energies." Throughout my hairstyling career I was able to help others by communicating with my clients through the mirror—empowering them to be self-reliant, and encouraging them to be responsible for their health by using natural remedies. I took pleasure in sharing my experiences and learning of natural healing with my clients as I was doing their hair. When I look back I am proud to see how many lives I have influenced just by sharing my knowledge. They saw how the natural healing was benefitting me and decided that instead of just going to see a doctor, they would see a homeopath as well. My gift was my ability to be inspired and to inspire others by being and living as an example, infusing within the circle of my clients the desire to explore alternative, natural therapies.

Before my mother passed away I had a health problem—a fibroid. No matter what I did, nothing helped, and my fibroid kept growing. At some point the fibroid grew so much, it became the size of a five-month fetus. I could feel it interfering with my organs, poisoning my body. Finally, it was my mother who suggested I have a hysterectomy. Despite my reliance on natural healing until that day, I accepted her suggestion, feeling I had exhausted all other options.

What I did not realize at the time was that what I needed was not necessarily physical curing, but rather emotional healing. At that time I was in a marriage that was clearly not working. I did not know how to handle the relationship and did not honor nor love myself enough. My fibroid was a manifestation of this.

During my post-surgery recovery, I continued with various natural healing modalities. One day I was exchanging different experiences about alternative healing methods with one of my clients, when she told me about an experience that her mother had with something called Reiki. I was intrigued by the story and went to see the Reiki practitioner myself. My first session more than met my expectations, and following my treatment, my recovery was so rapid that the doctors were amazed!

My first taste of Reiki was also my first introduction to spirituality. Until that day, I never really understood what spirituality meant. Following my first treatment, however, I was not only energized in a physical sense, but more importantly I was inspired by the flow of fresh ideas of what I wanted to do with my life.

I contacted the practitioner who treated me, who was also a teacher, and said to her, "I want to learn how you do this. Can I?"

She replied, "Yes, anyone can." That is how I came to start my first degree Reiki. During that time I was growing increasingly excited about the subject, convincing everyone around me to let me practice on them.

Then my mother passed away. Grief from my mother's death, which I could not process, had settled into my lower back. Although I had been having lower back problems since I first got married, I went from having mild pain to having a herniated disc within a month. I always thought standing on my feet for too long had caused it, but once again, that experience reminded me that behind my pain lay an emotional disconnect. Although the three months following my mother's death were accompanied by acute pain, the insight that the two were related was an eye-opening experience: I learned that physical pain signals a disconnection to the self. I learned to live with the pain without using painkillers. I learned to merge with it, accept it, and appreciate it—and to my surprise, the pain changed, and at times even dissipated. Looking back, I realize how much wisdom I have gained through this experience.

My marriage fell apart around the time of my mother's death, and in hindsight, I recognize that I was ready for this change to happen. I realized that I was not happy and not living to my full potential. I finally understood that I needed to let go of my old life and my old views of the world and myself. I also realized that despite my earlier beliefs, I was dispensable, even for my children who were aged 17, 22, and 27. They did not need me around full time, cooking and cleaning for them. They could manage just fine independently. I needed to focus more on myself.

My back pain brought me back to practicing Reiki, studying second and third degree Reiki. I re-enrolled in school, studying in the holistic program at the Transformational Arts College. Through my studies and my own personal healing, I got involved with Native healing traditions and shamanic work. I went to Peru twice on a shamanic journey. The first time I focused on self healing, understanding I had to let go of my own baggage before I could help others. When I finished my studies, I started working part time at a friend's homeopathic office, which was coincidentally at the same building as Pirjo's dental office. At that time, I was still debating whether I should quit my hairstyling career or not, since I still needed to make a living.

During my second trip to Peru, however, a window of opportunity opened. We were driving to a spiritual site one day, and while I was reading some passages from an inspirational book, all of my fears melted away, and it became clear to me that I was ready to set up an holistic practice and help others on a full-time basis.

Upon my return from Peru, I began searching for a place to set up my healing practice. Within two weeks I found an office in downtown Toronto. I practiced there for a year, but I felt that although it was a good starting point, it wasn't the right place for me. Before I left the office, however, I knew that I needed to learn not to be affected by my surroundings and to embrace the knowledge that I will be okay wherever I am. And then synchronicity kicked in. One day I noticed a sign for a space for lease in a neighboring building. I decided to call and inquire about the price and was told that the space was already leased, but that another space in a nearby building had just become available. To my surprise, it was the building I was already in! I met with the landlord and leased my new office, opening my own holistic center.

Recently I made another step in enhancing my spiritual growth. Once again, I needed a realization, and it came through a physical-health issue. It was through this health issue that I was prompted to once again reassess myself, and the way that I live my life, bringing opportunity for a huge step forward on my spiritual journey. Two years prior I discovered a lump in my breast. It was diagnosed as fibrotic tissue, and I was instructed to keep a watch on it. The year after, I went through a stressful period in my life concerning my children. Although I knew a lot about healing myself, my focus had shifted to my children, once again neglecting myself.

The lump in my breast began to grow, and I was scheduled for a mammogram. The procedure was extremely invasive, and it took two weeks for this part of my body to calm down. After this experience, I knew that even if the lump were diagnosed as cancerous, I would not undergo chemotherapy. Instead, I was going to put my faith in my knowledge of natural holistic healing and seek natural therapies to deal with it.

After the mammogram I was referred to do a biopsy. I was concerned, and put a lot of thought into it. I did not know whether or not it was cancerous at this point, but I knew that if I did not make the necessary changes in my life, it could be. What I needed was not a biopsy of my breast, but a biopsy of my life, my ideas, and my fears. I needed to love myself more deeply. I needed to love my breast. I started an internal dialogue with my lump and got the feeling that it did not want to be poked at or cut out. The message was clear: my health was acting up, signaling that I had to re-learn how to listen to myself, love myself, and let go of my fear. I needed to become my first priority, without feeling guilty about it.

I started making big changes in my life. Instead of undergoing a biopsy, I decided to travel to India and to return home only once I had put my life in order. When I did finally return, the people I met naturally assumed that since I was back, the lump was gone. The lump is actually still there. What is gone is my fear. I view my lump as my biggest teacher. I have accepted it. It allowed me the opportunity to really, fully, love myself.

Although it took over 20 years, I now understand why I had to undergo all these challenges in my life to get me to where I am today. Timing is everything, and you need to be ready for the things that await you. In spite of all of the knowledge I gained early in life, my physical body went through changes that I could not understand at that time. I had been focusing on only one part of myself, the physical body, while neglecting to pay attention to my emotional body, thus creating a disconnection from feeling whole. My main insight from these experiences, therefore, is that one cannot separate the physical, emotional, and spiritual body. We will move much more quickly in our journey as long as we honor all aspects of ourselves.

It was through the experience of putting my trust in traditional Western medicine, which turned out to be ineffective, that I gained the understanding that pain and disease cannot be feared and cut out since they will return in a different form. We cannot keep cutting off parts of ourselves and expect to feel healthy and whole! By focusing only on the discomfort of pain, by trying to mask it or hide from it, we only provoke mistrust in our own body's ability to heal. All we need is the ability to listen, feel and love, without the necessity to engage our reasoning mind. We need to trust that we are a part of God, the cosmic power that is unlimited and abundantly available to all of us. By focusing on and loving our own body, loving every part of our being, and recognizing our unlimited power, our body will begin to heal. It is this healing process that I bring and offer to my clients.

I personalize the healing process of my clients to whatever they may need at the time—taking them on a journey to feel God and to feel themselves through their different senses. The healing process may make use of various modalities. It may make use, for example, of the sense of hearing, by listening to the sounds around you and within you and becoming one with the vibration of sound. It may utilize the sense of sight, looking at the expansion of your world through your third eye. It may involve helping you realize that you are one with your breath, simply observing how it slows down, feeling it permeating every cell of your body, bringing with it love, life, and health. We may use the sense of smell, appreciating the aromas of essential oils and becoming one with the vibration of these oils during an aromatherapy lymphatic massage. Throughout the massage, I guide my clients to feel their body from head to toe, to feel the changes in their body without complaining—accepting and embracing each change, recognizing it as the life force flowing in and charging each cell of their body. In order to engage the healing process, one must accept the feeling of change in her body by focusing on the feelings it generates and loving it. One must accept her body as a part of God. By focusing on these feelings and accepting our body and change, we learn to embrace and love ourselves and to embrace God within us.

When you open up to energy healing, you access not only the physical body but also other levels of your being. Dreams are often an indicator of healing and release. I believe that the so-called "dream state" is not really a *dream* state. Who is to say what is reality or illusion? For example, following my first energy-healing treatment with Pirjo, she reported having an incredible dream. In this dream, Pirjo was peeing so much there seemed to be no end. Next, she was throwing up until there was nothing left to throw up. The same happened after our second session. Both times she woke up wondering if she was really sick—but she was not. Her dream was a manifestation of the cleansing work we had done together.

Through experiencing the different stages of my personal healing, I came to believe that I am meant to help others realize that they can help themselves. I want to make a difference, educating people as to what healing means, and how the body, mind, and soul can be healed. Being invited to Pirjo's practice to speak to the staff about the energy healing work I do was a rewarding experience. I realized how important it is to present to others the concepts of healing, how we can heal, and why we need to look at different aspects of healing. Networking and working together is essential in order to inspire, support, and give courage to one another. As women, we have a natural tendency to become the caretakers. We must remember, however, that to be able to care for others, we must first apply that caring to ourselves. I continuously learn how simple it really is. In many ways, my journey has only just begun.

—*Olina Budin*

You can learn more about Olina Budin at: www.puressence-inc.com

Cheryl Chabluk—Medium and Healer

Photo: Yanka Van der Kolk

Cheryl is one of the key members of my team, working at the energetic level as a medium and an intuitive coach. One of the main benefits I derive from my work with her is the clarity that her gifts generate. Synchronicity confirms that as well—I live on the 18th floor of my building and coincidentally, both times Cheryl and I were talking about clarity in my kitchen, the window cleaner appeared outside! Amazingly, I had never seen him before!

Cheryl is incredibly versatile. Aside from illuminating various situations in my life with her ability and vision, she has often assisted me in finding comfort, lucidity, and a fresh outlook on situations that are seemingly unchangeable. Cheryl has also enlightened me to see my attachments to objects and certain individuals for what they really are: emotional roadblocks in my path to happiness and success that prevent me from moving forward until I learn to detach myself from them.

One of the most important things I have learned from Cheryl is the importance of trusting and following my heart and core. She also taught me an easy technique to uncover what is in my heart and core, simply by making a decision, any decision, and being aware of my body's reaction to it and what emotions arise. The information I draw from this little exercise often answers my questions regarding my choices.

Although Cheryl uses a variety of methods in her work, together we mostly focus on several techniques which have assisted me greatly in clarifying my path and achieving my goals: Tarot card reading, Reiki healing, and mantra chanting. Utilizing these tools allows me to receive information I am seeking or may need at the moment, and which I can use for my personal healing, growth, and decision-making. Furthermore, Cheryl has equipped me with helpful tools such as rune stones, angel cards, and Native Medicine cards that I can utilize on my own when facing emotionally challenging situations. These tools are simple ways to receive information and messages that can be interpreted to gain different perspectives and valuable insight into situations.

The information Cheryl shares with me has always been true, even if I cannot know it at the time. On many occasions I have reviewed situations in retrospect—situations in which I was uncertain of which direction to take, only to realize that Cheryl had known all along! These incidents continuously reinforce my trust in her.

What amazes me most about Cheryl is how in tune she is with her clients. Besides myself, other people in my office meet and consult with her as well. What is unique about Cheryl is that from time to time, one of us may feel anxious or perplexed by a certain situation or dilemma, and when we really need her support and input, she just appears! Cheryl's openness to non-verbal, telepathic communication is so advanced that she simply knows when we are in need of her guidance!

—Pirjo Friedman

Each person in this world has infinite possibilities in life, and although I believe we can all achieve our goals—whatever they may be—we may at times need guidance in order to stay on our path and move along it successfully. That is the role of our team: to provide us with the help and advice we need. Even if we are not aware of it, we all work with a team, both physical and spiritual, at all times. What we sometimes lack is the courage to reach out and ask for help. The easiest way of receiving this help is by inviting people to surround you in your life, guide you, and fill you with confidence in what you do. Your team, however, need not be limited to the physical world! Be courageous—you can work with a bigger team!

My gift is being able to hear, smell, and feel the invisible team. I consider myself an extension of a spiritual family up above. I believe that the synergy of God, our ancestors, the angels, and the saints have created the earth, and that we are all a part of that spiritual family. I feel fortunate to be able to connect and communicate with the family above, and channel messages to others here on earth.

I usually begin my work with clients by teaching them to trust themselves, their emotions and core feelings. The second step involves getting them to trust others. It is important to cultivate a relationship with the members of your team and develop confidence that they will never lead you astray. Establishing trust is absolutely vital in order to maximize our benefit from the team.

Trusting your team, however, is not enough, because believing that they will lead you in the right direction does not guarantee that you will accept their guidance. One must remain open to receiving messages from the team and remember that messages can come from everywhere and anywhere. Turn on the television, open a magazine, read the roadside advertisements while you are sitting in traffic—there is something there for you to notice! Being open to messages from your team will help you reach new levels of awareness, whether the issues you deal with relate to your work, personal relationships, financial situation, or anything else. During my work with Pirjo we attempted to reach this level of openness and awareness with her staff. Pirjo recognized the importance of such work, since if employees are able to deal effectively with their various situations, whether work related or personal, and move forward in their lives, the overall energy and efficiency of the practice improves.

Being receptive is important even when I am the one channeling the messages. When I work with someone, I step outside my body, and therefore I am not aware and cannot remember the messages I deliver. It is the responsibility of the person with me to be open to these messages, to listen and absorb them. For this reason, I always recommend taping my sessions. It is impossible to hear and absorb everything at one time—some things we are simply not ready to hear. Taping the session, however, captures its energy, and the client can listen to it later when she is ready to hear and accept the messages.

Being open and receptive also allows my clients to communicate with me. When someone is experiencing a challenge, I can often feel and hear it. If this person needs me to appear, I will. All they need to do is be open to telepathic vibrations; otherwise I will not be able receive the message.

Once they are stronger from gaining confidence in themselves and in their team, I lead my clients to the next step: "the marking of their path." By having my clients face the question, "*Where do I wish to go*?" we gain valuable insight into the ultimate goal they aspire to achieve. Defining what success means to you is essential—once you know where you are going, the path to get there will naturally reveal itself.

I trust that if people truly believe and focus on what they desire and where they want to be, they will get their wish, no matter what. There is no obstacle they cannot remove, and no reason for them to stop. Challenges along the way are simply blessings in disguise. Any desire or goal one may have is always created due to a certain lack or block. If there were no challenges in achieving our wishes, we would not need to wish for them! Therefore, it is important to see challenges for what they really are: opportunities that will advance us to the next level by helping us define what it is we truly desire. I can assist in achieving this clarity as well. My work usually involves listening to the goals and wants of my clients and helping them open the pathway to their goals. I do this by removing any obstacles that may be preventing them from reaching their next step through coaching, channeling messages from our spiritual guides and through energy healing.

Obstacles do not arise only in the form of obvious challenges, however. One disguised form of obstacles that is quite common is attachment, whether to others or to objects. These attachments are often based on insecurity: the fear of moving forward into the unknown. We are afraid of being alone, of not having support or not receiving permission or approval from someone, and when scared we tend to hang onto what we have for reassurance—it is definitely more comforting than facing the unknown! Some people hold on so tightly to these attachments they come to the point of suffering.

In order to transform these attachments to stepping-stones rather than obstacles in your path one must first face these fears by acknowledging them and taking responsibility for them. Recognize the fear—what are you dreading and why? Acquaint yourself with the fear—when does it arise, what form does it take? Analyze the fear—what is the source of the fear? What attachments does it generate? Be honest with yourself—why can you not let it go? Understanding every aspect of our fear will make it familiar, and what is familiar can no longer be frightening! Furthermore, realizing that attachments are merely manifestations of these fears allows you to finally detach and release yourself from them. Surrendering attachments, fears, and other confining aspects of our lives allows us to open our energy in new directions, invite new things into our lives, and clear our path in our journey to achieve our goals.

Physical problems are often manifestations of emotional issues as well, and while physical healing can come in the form of treatment, there are other, more natural ways of healing. My grandmother taught me that you can and should talk to your body parts, and there you will find a solution. By communicating with your body on the emotional level and treating pain with homeopathy, it is possible to restore health and comfort in situations where most people will end up in the hospital. For example, knee problems may arise from problems with flexibility or stability. Communicate with your knee; express your appreciation and attentiveness; be grateful that the pain is raising your awareness to a more fundamental problem. Then take a look at your life, examine your relationships, find where you are feeling powerless, overpowered, or off balance. The solution will come shortly, along with your recovery.

Once my clients have established trust and openness with their teams, and once they have defined their path, I assist them through my readings, with the aim of providing them with awareness of their options. There are many tools I can use to awaken my senses as to channel information from the spiritual side. Some of these tools are crystal balls or tea leaves. I may become clairvoyant, depending on how I feel. Another tool I use often is Tarot cards. As I shuffle the deck, my touch passes energies into the cards—it is magical. The cards then provide whatever information or answers you are looking for. I use a different deck based on where my client is in their life. I have special decks for romance, relationships, work, or whatever other aspect I feel drawn to. Many of these tools you can use on your own. For example, try "scrying"—gaze into a pool of water in a dark bowl and see what appears to you. It's easy! Simply ask a question, and you will visually see an image in the water or in your mind.

While the messages may help illuminate various situations, it is solely the client's responsibility to make a choice that they feel good about. In a process of life experience there are no wrong decisions. But the question remains: what is the right decision? I believe that whatever choice you make, you have made the right one, as long as it feels right. If it feels like you have had too much cookie dough, that is probably a sign that the answer is no. No one can tell you what is right for you other than yourself. Even in hindsight, if you feel you are hitting walls and having problems, a situation is always rectifiable, and it is never too late. People may think that by working with someone like me, who possesses psychic abilities, means the future is predetermined. It certainly is not. Anytime you make a choice in your life, you recreate your future. With every decision, we simply start from a new place.

During my work with clients I often assign them certain tasks, a technique I learned from my grandmother. Back in her day, if you were sick you would show up at my grandmother's door, and she would instruct you to do something unusual. Each person received a different prescription. The energy you put into completing the task has the power to change reality. For example, I once instructed Pirjo to place one white, long-stemmed rose in a vase in her home in order to generate peace and calm. Another time I instructed her to buy pearls, as they represent nurturing and protection of our spiritual essence. Sometimes it may not make a lot of sense, but if that is what the ancestors and spirits are asking for, then that is what needs to be done. They will see your effort and will reward you for it.

I love working with my healing energies. It has certainly allowed me a fascinating journey! I have seen amazing things, assisted people out of wheelchairs, and healed people considered terminal. My journey, however, has not been without challenges: I fought against people who urged me to give up my dream and pursue a "real job." I am the first Reiki master to work within a hospital, although at first they did not accept me, forcing me to battle for a long time before I realized that dream. By reaching that goal, however, I managed to open the doors of hospitals for Reiki healers, reflexologists, and other natural healers. My early twenties were my roughest years, as a mother to a newborn baby and having an injured husband who could neither walk nor work. Seeing my husband suffering in pain, I resolved that no matter what, I was going to find the way to heal him. And I did, using my Reiki healing abilities and strong faith.

My philosophy throughout these rough times was to focus on my goals and dreams. As I reached each of them, it was time to move on to the next level. At the core, life's experiences are truly about those moments of pure joy and inspiration—moments you never want to end. Our paths are meant to lead us there. If we stop ourselves along the way, it is only because of our fear. However, if you let go of your frustration and remain open to the guidance of your team, your solution will appear in one form or another.

Every journey is individual and unique—no two people are alike. However, as part of my work with people I teach them the three basic laws of the universe that lie at the beginning of each journey. First, the Law of Attraction, which means that the universe will respond to whatever vibration you create by awarding you more of what you are vibrating. Second, the Law of Conscious

Creation, which means that you draw into your life whatever you devote your mind, energy, and focus to. And third, the Law of Allowing, which promotes the riddance of doubt and hesitation from our lives. By learning to master these laws, one can start putting things into motion in life, in the journey towards realizing goals.

Believe in yourself. Be inspired, since we create something with every moment of our lives. Do not be afraid to ask for everything you want: love, money, relationships, a career… If you ask for it, it will come to you. Think of it like Christmas. When I was a child, I would take Christmas very seriously. My mother would ask me what I would like to get for the holidays, and I would start looking through books and magazines and discussing it with my friends—I would not stop thinking about it! I believe that every day of our life can be Christmas morning. The non-physical world is asking you, "What do you want?" And if we do not know what it is that we want, we should actively search for it.

—Cheryl Chabluk

Marlene Durrell—
Executive Business Coach

Photo: Yanka Van der Kolk

Marlene and I first met at an Association for Creative Change in Organization Renewal and Development meeting when I was searching for new ways to lead my team as president of the Women Entrepreneurs of Canada (WEC) organization. Marlene offered to discuss how I could build my teams, both at my dental practice and at WEC. During our first meeting it was clear to me that this relationship was one I wanted to pursue. I later asked Marlene to serve on the board of WEC as treasurer during my tenure as president. Over time, we developed a strong connection both personally and professionally.

Marlene's diverse abilities and achievements make her an effective leadership and business coach, organizational-development consultant, and trainer. Over the years I have benefitted greatly from her services, in both one-on-one coaching sessions and in-group consultation sessions with my staff, colleagues, and friends, all aimed at enhancing the marketing of oneself in business.

DR. PIRJO FRIEDMAN, D.D.S.

Marlene has assisted me through various transition periods in my life by creating clarity, particularly when personal issues overlapped or were spilling into my professional, business life. One of the major issues we worked through related to some negative behavioral patterns I had adopted over time. For example, for many years I could not trust people and relationships, being suspicious of everyone and everything. I was continuously attracting certain types of people and relationships into my life, which were harmful to me, generating drama, chaos, and fear. I continued doing this because on some level I was actually getting something out of the emotional upheaval—it made me feel alive. I can trace this pattern to my youth, to times when I experienced such strong emotional pain that I even contemplated suicide. I have always had very strong energies, and when I did not control them they were sometimes channeled in negative directions.

Through my work with Marlene, I came to realize that without resolving these behavioral patterns, I could never fully heal and move on in other aspects of my life. I began to see how my suspicion tended to rise until I began to communicate about it. Conversation enabled me to see the bigger picture, and I could therefore determine whether my suspicions were real, generated by my intuition, or whether they were merely an illusion. Naturally, being able to release these feelings of suspicion in my relationships, both at work and in my personal life, has enabled me to grow as a person and live a drama-free life. I learned how to effectively handle my energies, channeling them to more productive outlets, such as manifesting my goals.

Through our sessions, Marlene also assisted me in preparing for the next steps in my life: the selling of my practice and the building of my new business. She ensured that I continued to think forward, even though I had yet to find a buyer for my practice. She encouraged me to take the steps necessary to reach my ultimate goals and to overcome my fears about this transition: the fear of no longer being a dentist, which has become a part of my identity; the fear of not having the structure and routine I had had in my life for over 30 years; and the fear of not having the authority when people ask for my advice as a dentist.

Marlene's work continuously reinforces my conviction in the importance of one's team. There is a limit to how much you can achieve when you do things by yourself. Marlene's mission statement is: "To create inspiring environments for learning, growth and achievement." This is exactly what I feel we have achieved in our work together.

—Pirjo Friedman

Today's business environment has changed. It is leaner, with less top-down decision-making and increased reliance on individuals and teams to self-manage and add value. Collaboration and co-operation rather than competition are becoming the requisite skills for success. The main focus of my business, The Walmsley Group Inc., is on creating higher levels of organizational effectiveness and improving the bottom line, through coaching and consulting.

As an executive and business coach, I specialize in coaching executives and managers for improved individual and organizational results. I do this by assisting my clients and the members of their organization to identify the personal and organizational goals, objectives, and strategies necessary to achieve the organization's mission and vision. Through coaching, I help clients to clarify the implications of the organizational goals for their own growth and development. I encourage them to align their business objectives with their personal objectives so that they can achieve their own goals while performing at a high level for the organization. In addition, we collaborate to develop proactive strategies both for their personal growth and the growth of the business.

Aside from my focus on coaching, I also consult with companies on various human resources and organizational development issues, such as change management, team development, strategic planning, and employment and development strategies. I am also the founder of a virtual organization of professionals, whose goal is to form strategic partnerships in order to achieve business and personal success. Throughout my career, I have worked with *for*-profit and *not-for*-profit organizations, both internally and externally.

The essence of my work is helping clients and their teams increase their awareness and clarity of who they are and where they want to be. Most people who turn to me wish to get more out of their lives and their careers—they know they are ready to move on, but are not certain how to get there. By partnering with me, I am able to assist them in defining exactly where it is they want to go, and how they want to get there.

As opposed to therapy, which is all about peeling off layers and going back into the past to understand how one got to where one is, the work I do with my clients is about "becoming." Sometimes this involves introspective examination to understand what brought you to where you are so you know what to change. More frequently, however, it involves clarifying where you want to be and who you need to be to get there. Once you define your goals, things around you will start to happen, and consequentially, the steps required to get there will become clearer. It is important to remember, however, that these steps are not set in stone—they may change along the way. As you observe the events around you unfolding over time, the actions required to reach your goals evolve organically.

When Pirjo and I first started working together, her goal was to develop her management proficiency in working through change and her new endeavors and in creating a highly performing team in her practice. At the time, she already had a clear personal strategic plan and a strong idea of where she was headed and what steps were required to get her there. Therefore, my work with Pirjo focused more on her personal identity and relationships than on her business.

Some of the major issues Pirjo and I worked through in our sessions were related to the relationships in her life, particularly at her practice. My aim was to help Pirjo become aware of how the dynamics in her practice were shaping her relationships there and the relationships with others around her. I helped her examine her interactions and take notice of the similarities between all her relationships; for example, how she was continuously inviting the same type of people and relationships into her life. We discovered that Pirjo often took the role of the caretaker, inviting the type of people and relationships that she needed to carry on her shoulders, which resulted in stress and pain. Over time, as Pirjo understood and accepted this pattern and its consequences, she was able to clear these relationships and this tendency out of her life.

Another concern we dealt with was Pirjo's tendency to be suspicious of others. During the sessions in which we focused on this aspect of her life, I would ask Pirjo a series of questions geared to uncover what purpose her suspicion served her on a subconscious level. Perhaps it was not suspicion, but simply sharp intuition? Perhaps the suspicion was triggered by a more basic emotion such as fear? Very often suspicion is a manifestation of fear, and it can also act as a self-fulfilling prophecy. If we fear that someone is going to pull away from us, we manifest this fear into suspicion that they will not come through for us, and eventually they will not!

You cannot get to where you want to go by staying where you are! You must be willing to let go in order to get what you want. Setting new goals in your life, regarding who you want to be or where you would like to get to, is a helpful tool for letting go of your old goals, behaviors, relationships and life. Pirjo, for example, eventually managed to let go of her practice, despite all her fears and reservations about no longer being a dentist, by focusing on her new endeavors as a businesswoman and writer. Letting go of her practice has enabled her to see her relationships more clearly, enabling her to decide either to release them or enhance them. Pirjo cleared out the papers, relationships, and other possessions that she no longer needed in the clinic to make room for new things. Once this physical and emotional space is available, new things can and *will* start to happen.

Letting go of the negative aspects in her life has allowed Pirjo to become much lighter, as opposed to the heaviness she had been dragging with her for many years. By redefining and recreating herself, Pirjo no longer needed to hold on to her old ways of being, and was finally able to release the negative relationships and behavior patterns of her past and focus her strong energies into pursuing and manifesting her new goals.

Every person I have worked with is different. People have different ways of dealing with and sorting out their issues, and they are ready to do so at different times. However, when people pay attention to their body-mind connection and stick with their gut instincts it makes a big difference. Another commonality is that changing your way of thinking is a prerequisite for change, for getting to a new level in your life or in your career. Through coaching, I equip my clients with the questions that they need to understand and challenge, and through this process, they can change their way of thinking.

Trust that when something, *anything*, shows up in your life, it is there to serve a purpose for you. It is there for you to learn from. This is particularly true for our team and our relationships with them. Throughout our lives, we encounter and interact with people possessing varied talents and abilities. We need them all, every piece of the puzzle, in order to create our complete picture, our world—this cannot be done by the individual alone. One must not fear inviting the people they need into their lives. After all, we can only know ourselves in relation to others. Without you, there *is* no me.

—*Marlene Durrell*

You can learn more about Marlene Durrell at: www.thewalmsleygroup.com

Sharon Hay—Feng Shui Practitioner

Photo: Yanka Van der Kolk

Sharon and I first met at a Christmas party through a business acquaintance, and we later served together on the Board of the Women Entrepreneurs of Canada organization. When we met Sharon had just begun her career in Feng Shui, and I soon realized that we could both benefit extensively from one another. I wished to work with Sharon in order to focus the energy and create an optimal environment in my home, investment properties, and business. I soon recognized Sharon's talent and sought other friends and acquaintances that could use her skills.

My main purpose when working with Sharon was enhancing the relationships, health, and success in my home and business, as well as preparing my investment properties for sale. Sharon succeeded in creating optimal energies in these spaces, working with what I already had. Indeed, soon after she stepped in, I managed to sell both properties for my asking price!

Working with Sharon I learned that objects carry energy. Certain objects can create symbolic energies, which can be used to attract specific things in life. What I found interesting is that these energies can be changed. Placing various objects or using certain colors, for example, create specific desired effects. For instance, while examining my home, Sharon recommended placing a rug in the entrance hall. This simple addition had the effect of welcoming people into my home. When I walked into the apartment for the first time after the carpet had been added I could really feel the change. In addition to this, Sharon and I allocated different spaces in the apartment for various themes such as travel, recognition, wealth, and so forth. In my study, for example, I created the "fame corner." In this space I keep the manuscripts for my books along with photographs of influential people I have met over the years, with the purpose of enhancing my own success.

Aside from Sharon's valuable suggestions in the redecorating process, she has also taught me to stay tuned to personal changes or changes in the circumstances surrounding me, stressing the importance of reflecting these changes in my space and environment. And indeed, over the years, major life changes, such as retiring from dental practice or the termination of a romantic relationship, as well as minor changes, such as a newfound interest have been marked by various changes in my home and office—changes, which I intuitively felt, must take place.

—Pirjo Friedman

I am the type of person that *requires* change. I try to learn as much as I can from whatever I am doing at a time and must then move on to use that experience in my next project or job. Some people tease me about my need for variation, saying, "Oh, you are always after the next shiny thing that comes along!" I simply laugh it off. My life is always evolving; I am always growing and learning. As I move forward through my life, I am always shedding the skin, letting go of things that no longer serve me, moving onto the next new adventure, and sharing the things I learn along the way.

A few years ago I was in the computer industry, but always had other interests in things like home renovation, real estate, and decorating. The building and decoration of houses and the way they enhance people's lives fascinated me. I loved showing homes to people, decorating, and putting the finishing touches that gave the houses personality. I especially liked matching up the personality of the house to that of the owner. Aside from all these, I was also involved with some marketing and advertising aspects of the business, another occupation I enjoyed immensely, particularly identifying and promoting whatever it is that people desire. The bottom line was that I simply took pleasure in helping people by fulfilling their needs. Later I found that Feng Shui does all this as well.

Looking back, I appreciate how numerous experiences have all led me to the practice of Feng Shui. Several years ago I consulted with two separate psychics, both of whom commented on my occupation. According to both, I was meant to be doing something with healing. When I mentioned I had been working with computers for the past ten years, they claimed that they did not find any indication of this in their readings. This confirmed my personal feeling that aside from allowing me to pay my bills, my occupation no longer suited or interested me.

Soon after this revelation, other paths began to appear, leading me to my new profession. Several years ago, the universe had suddenly begun throwing hints at me, focusing my attention on Feng Shui. Books on the subject were recommended to me; I would turn on the television and a Feng Shui program would be on, or I would browse through a magazine and spot an article or an ad on the topic. Finally, the *idea* of Feng Shui hit me and resonated. I got the message: I needed to learn *more* about Feng Shui.

The more I learned, the more I realized that I had already intuitively understood many of the concepts involved with Feng Shui and yet the exposure to all this new information pieced everything together for me—how we affect our environment, and how our environment is affecting us. While reading any material I could get my hands on, I started putting my newly acquired knowledge of Feng Shui into practice, making changes in my own home and observing the effects. Once I began practicing Feng Shui, the energies started moving and life began to flow better. I continuously received confirmation that I was heading in the right direction.

I decided to pursue a career in Feng Shui, beginning my formal education at a school in California. However, I could not imagine how I would come up with the $3,000 fee for the course as well as the travel and accommodation costs. Despite this challenge, I believed that if this was truly the path I was meant to pursue then things would work out. And indeed I came up with the money quite quickly. Everything worked out, and I thought to myself, *Is that a sign or what?*

Once I finished school, I returned to Toronto and started practicing. At first I practiced on my friends, whom I considered my most critical reviewers. Not all of them were into Feng Shui, though. While some were open to the idea, others said, "Sharon, that is a crock!" But once my job was done, all of them came back excited, and said, "You will never believe what happened!" Out of the blue, things just started happening to them. Long-awaited changes in different aspects of their lives finally began to take place. The feedback I received from my friends confirmed once and for all that I had found my calling. I established my business and began practicing full time with the help of some acquaintances, like Pirjo. She connected me with several potential clients, and although at first I was hesitant and worried that I might not be ready, she insisted I call them.

The art of Feng Shui is all about energies. As we learned in school, there is energy in everything—everything is made of molecules bouncing against each other; everything is continuously moving. The Chinese have known this for over six thousand years. Feng Shui is based on the fact that objects contain energies, as do houses. That is why it is so important, for example, to inquire who the previous owners of a house were before purchasing it, and why it is sometimes risky to wear other people's jewelry, since old jewelry may hold negative energies.

An important aspect of Feng Shui is identifying what "energy blockers" exist in a certain environment and figuring out a way of removing them in order to continue our journey in life in a positive way. I find that since the completion of my studies and the beginning of my practice of Feng Shui, my intuition in general and my ability to sniff out other people's energy blockages in particular has advanced significantly. For example, once I was standing in a restaurant, uncertain of what to order. I was peeking at other people's plates around me, and finally said to the waitress, "I will have what the artist in the corner is having."

"Oh Timmy, do you know Timmy?" she asked.

I did not. Instead I replied, "I don't know his name, but I know he has something interesting on his plate."

The waitress asked how I knew the man was an artist, but I could not tell her. I did not know how I knew. The words had simply come out of my mouth.

My intuition has been very helpful in my practice. For example, I often walk into a client's home, notice an object, and inquire about the story behind it. I can feel that the object is somehow unrelated, and indeed, soon find out that it was a gift, or ended up in its place by some odd circumstance. In the same way, I can sense my clients' blockages in their lives and spaces. Many of the questions I ask a client when we first meet may seem very personal, and are therefore not always easy to ask; but through this information I can pick up the blockages and issues of my clients, which we will later need to work through. Sometimes mental blockages manifest into their physical surroundings and vice versa.

Feng Shui prescribes various methods of removing blockages and improving the energies in a given space. In Pirjo's home, for example, some spaces lacked energy while others had an abundance of rushing energy. In order to create balance, we used crystals, which are often used to regulate energy. Crystals are effective since they speed up the energy in spaces where there is difficulty of getting the energy to flow, and slow down the energy in long narrow spaces where it is shooting through too fast. It is essential that the energy meander around the entire space of the apartment, house or office. If it simply shoots through in a straight line, it will not flow into all of the rooms effectively. Bedrooms are especially vulnerable to unbalanced energy. If there is too much energy moving in and out, this may disturb people's sleep because their bodies feel the energy's movement, and their mind will always be racing. This was exactly the case with the room of Pirjo's youngest daughter. In these cases I often suggest carpeting if there is only hardwood flooring, at least around the bed if not in the entire room, in order to stop the energy from shooting past. Another tool is placing something soft about the bed, such as a calming picture on the wall.

One of the Feng Shui Principles is that there are five elements, or categories, of energy: fire, water, metal, earth, and wood. There are thousands of items in each category and each element relates differently to other elements in every category. The balance of all five elements in a room and throughout the home is necessary to ensure harmony and peacefulness.

People and animal spirits are the most powerful elements of energy on earth, as they symbolize the fire element—the strongest, fastest, and most powerful of the five elements. That is how several people gathered together and thinking collectively about a certain thing can move mountains, so to speak! Therefore, when Pirjo declared her ambitions for her books and her practice, we placed pictures of people and animal objects in a certain area, which we designated as the fame and recognition area, with the aim of energizing that space. The fire element in general and the fame and recognition area in particular were further enhanced by pyramid shapes and red and pink colors. Pink is used to enhance the relationship area as well. Romance can be enhanced in bedrooms by placing things in pairs to strengthen relationship energy. It is important to ensure that bedside tables and lamps are always at the same height on both sides of the bed in order to promote equality in the relationship.

Another aspect that required attention in Pirjo's home related to the water element. Having too much of the water element is not ideal since it throws the elemental balance off. But this was the situation in Pirjo's bathrooms, where mirrors, toilets, sinks, metals and other shiny surfaces represented an abundance of water. I suggested that Pirjo cure the problem by adding things from the wood element, such as flowers and plush carpets or mats, since wood absorbs the water element and helps moderate it.

Feng Shui does not only apply for decoration. In my practice of Feng Shui I often incorporate my old career in computers, allowing me to save considerable amounts of money by creating my own websites. In turn, I integrate Feng Shui principles in my websites, placing my logos in certain areas and using various colors and textures to enhance and direct the energy and generate more life in the website.

As a Feng Shui consultant, I am typically not the one making the changes. I make suggestions and raise ideas, and sometimes I help the client choose the furniture, decorations, and other articles. However, when redecorating your own space, each object should appeal to you and your tastes; you should feel good about it, and through that, energize it with positive energy. You should be able, at the end of the day, to look around your home or office and enjoy what you are seeing.

Feng Shui is also about energizing your objects by *using* them, by incorporating them in your daily life. For example, music and musical instruments are always a valuable addition in any room; however, keep in mind that musical instruments are meant to be played, not just to sit around collecting dust. For this reason I always use my good china, which some may think is too nice to be used. It makes me happy, and I feel the dishes are happier as they are being used and fulfilling the purpose for which they were created. If you have good dishes and crystal—use them. You are worth it! Remember, things that just sit on a shelf for years create stale energy in your home and thus in your life.

It is important to realize the finality of certain parts and aspects of your life, as this will generate changes in your home and office. If you are no longer interested in a certain theme, for example, make sure that the articles associated with it are removed. The removal of aspects of your life that are no longer relevant will allow for new energies and opportunities to replace them. For example, it is advisable that anything pertaining to your career and which you would like to energize be placed in the front of the house. However, if you are retiring and intend for your career to start winding down—place it at the back. Set aside the space in the front of the house for objects that symbolize your plans for your retirement, or any other interests that are grabbing your attention at this time.

It is also important to remember to trust that the universe will serve you in ways you may not imagine. When you enhance certain areas in specific directions, you cannot always know how things will develop. For example, I was once called in by a woman to enhance her marriage that was failing. Together, we worked on moving the energy around in the relationship area. Soon after, however, her husband left her. Devastated and angry, the client blamed me for ruining her marriage. I explained to her that in our work together she created the energy in a way that would be most positive for her. Perhaps the consequences were meant to awaken her and to make her realize that it was time for her to move on.

To conclude, one must remember that Feng Shui and the rearrangement of your home and office may not be enough to create the changes you want to see in your life. Even if the energies in your home are flowing, you must leave your home in order to meet the people who will actively get things going in your life. When you step outside your doorstep—going to work, the store, your doctor, the dentist or wherever—you will meet these people. They could be your employees, boss, co-workers, bank manager or accountant—anyone. For example, you may need a new car and discover that the person you happened to talk with during your wait in the bank is looking to sell one. The connection is made. When you go out into the world, sending out your energy regarding your goals and wishes—that is when the energy begins to flow, and synchronicity comes into play

—Sharon Hay

You can learn more about Sharon Hay at: www.fengshuihay.ca or www.torontofengshui.ca

Jeannie Mackay—
Family Counsellor and Author

Photo: Yanka Van der Kolk

Jeannie and I first met through the Women Entrepreneurs of Canada organization. Since then, I have consulted with her on several occasions with the purpose of promoting clarification and healing in my life. For the most part, our work has focused on understanding why I do what I do in certain situations, and on resolving several relationships that have caused me confusion, emotional turmoil, and pain.

I usually book my appointments with Jeannie well ahead of time, although I may not have a pressing need at the time. Just before my appointment date, however, things will suddenly begin to happen. By the time I go to see Jeannie, I really need to see her! When we meet, Jeannie and I work quite intensely on a number of issues. Once we establish the order of priorities, we determine what methods and tools will be most appropriate.

Jeannie has helped me greatly in dealing with my worst fear: public speaking. Through our work together, I have gradually gained the confidence to face it and the belief that confronting our fears provides us with the best opportunities to grow and improve ourselves. Another major issue I have worked through with Jeannie has been the breakup of my most recent relationship. Our aim was to deal with the breakup in a way that would allow me to move beyond the sadness, the yearning for things to have turned out differently, and the hope of reuniting with him. I wanted to move forward in my life, and Jeannie helped me achieve this.

Working with Jeannie has contributed greatly to my healing process. For the first time in my life I realize that I do not have to repeat the same behaviors and relationships over and over again, nor do I have to suffer and be unhappy. I acquired the tools I need in order to deal with these issues and move forward. This knowledge awards me with the confidence that my fears can be conquered, that my next relationship will be different, and that my life will be different—that it will be better. I never know how the change will come about when I wish for it—we can never know how things will unfold. But one thing is for sure: the change will come.

—Pirjo Friedman

What I do, in a nutshell, is help people change their lives by guiding them through the retrieval, rebuilding, restoration, and healing of their soul. A part of this process is coming to understand why we repeatedly find ourselves in certain situations. Once we reveal the core issues underlying these patterns, we can resolve them, let them go, and move forward in our lives.

While some people require more time to speak about their issues and release their emotions, others do not. My sessions, therefore, do not have a time frame—they last as long as it takes to make a change. I will not let clients out the door until I can see in their eyes that they have shifted. Only then do I send them home to begin the process of integrating the change.

In order to work effectively with my clients, it is essential that I approach them in a way that they understand. For this I must be able to enter that person's model of the world. Some people are more receptive to certain ideas than others, for example. While some are open and curious about spirituality and the unseen, others require a more practical and hands-on approach, avoiding talk about spirituality and remaining within the concepts of their known world. While some are interested in talking about God, others get really upset if I do. I once had a client who got up, picked up her coat and said, "I'm leaving now," after I mentioned the word "God." Ultimately, she stayed for the session and we simply called God "innate intelligence" instead! On the other hand, other people get upset if you don't talk enough about God. For this reason it is imperative for me to tread carefully, being attentive to my clients' needs, beliefs, and opinions, in order to work with them effectively and achieve a deep rapport. For example, one of my previous clients suffered from schizophrenia. She came in, sat down, and said, "My refrigerator talks to me." The ticking and clicking sounds of electronic instruments can bother people who are seriously mentally ill. I had two ways of proceeding at that point; I could say, "Nonsense, refrigerators don't talk!" in which case I would have lost rapport with her; or I could say, "What does it say?" In my world refrigerators don't talk, but in her world they do!

Occasionally, I have clients come in and reveal that they are considering suicide. In these cases I never say, "Oh no, you can't do that! Don't even talk about it!" Instead I say, "Oh, now that's interesting. Do you have pills saved up or a gun or a noose or a hose for the exhaust of the car? How are you planning to do it?" My response is devoid of any judgmental reaction. "When are you going to do it? Where? Will you do it at the cottage or at your house? Now let's just think about this for a minute. What would happen if your six-year-old were the one to find you?" This is when it starts to connect with them that suicide is a permanent solution to a temporary problem. By talking about the little details, people seem to realize the finality and magnitude of their actions. Over the years, I have had quite a few clients who have talked about suicide, but none of them has actually gone through with it. They found another solution. As a councilor, I need to understand and relate to my client's model of the world in order to begin creating a familiar, comfortable, and safe space for them to begin their progress and healing. It is most important to pace first and then lead.

The work I do with my clients is not emotional work. Rather, it is mental work. The issues we work with may be emotional ones, but the work required to resolve them is not. In my sessions, I work with a variety of methods and tools, which I tailor to each client's needs and preferences. The main tool underlying my work, however, is my intuition. Over the years and through my work with people, I have learned that if I simply relax and allow things to flow naturally my intuition becomes a powerful tool. At times I will ask a client a question or propose that we imagine a certain situation, to which the client might respond, "How did you know?" I don't know how I know. Somehow my intuition enables me to sense certain things.

One technique I often use is Neuro-Linguistic Programming (NLP). NLP consists of various techniques, axioms, and beliefs that may be used for behavioral modification and personal development. This is done by continuously changing the client's linguistic and behavioral patterns, thus changing their beliefs and behavior until they reach the results they seek.

Another method I use is Holographic Repatterning. The assumption of this healing technique is that underneath any manifestation of a problem, be it physical or emotional pain, lies an underlying issue, or energy block, which must be recognized, acknowledged, and removed. The healing process includes the identification of one's issues through dialogue and muscle testing—a technique used to tap our body's intelligence and through that reveal information from our subconscious. Muscle testing uses the client's arm, leg, or any other muscle, to check the body's responses to various sentences. The muscles either lock or go weak against pressure, indicating a positive or a negative response from the unconscious. This is a very effective tool, since our body knows things that we may not consciously know, and it tells the truth. The process of Holographic Repatterning regards the body as a sculpture of light that sometimes, because of earlier experiences, vibrates at a less than optimal frequency. Another metaphor I use to explain this work is that the client's body is the hardware of a computer: their mind is the software of a computer, and I am the virus scanner. This brilliant process includes numerous different healing techniques that require very simple, almost childlike actions in order to change the hologram. For example, I may ask the client to do special breathing patterns, eye or body movements, make peculiar sounds, or look at pictures of flowers or various geometric shapes. It may seem strange at first, but doing these things can change one's frequencies in a very simple and effective way and restore their sculpture of light to optimal frequency.

Another method I employ is the examination of past lives. This is an extremely effective tool for healing and personal development. For example, my client may have a problem with a certain person, and judging by the information we have from this lifetime, this conflict is not based on anything substantial. In cases such as this, I can reveal whether the two have had a relationship in a previous lifetime, and what happened in that relationship that may cause the present conflict. Whether one believes in past lives or not, the explanations and results are amazing! With those who do not believe in it, or are not interested in dealing with it, I will say that I am using my imagination. For them, this information is imaginary, and yet the results can be as effective as with clients who do believe in past lives. Several years ago, a teenager came to see me because he was feeling alienated. I saw that in a past life he was from Pluto, and told him so. This explained why he was feeling so alienated! Since he was now on planet earth, I suggested that he might as well get used to being a teenage earthling and do the things teenage earthlings do! He went back to school, did his homework, found a girlfriend, and was happy.

Throughout my work with Pirjo, we have used many of the tools I have described in our efforts over several sessions to deal with the breakup of her recent relationship. In any relationship, there is an energetic line that connects people. When trying to let go of a relationship, it is helpful to think of this energetic line as a cord, and simply cut the cord in order to move on. Once you do this, you can open yourself up to new relationships. Our first session, therefore, was aimed at enabling Pirjo to sever the ties with her partner. We were careful not to do this in an angry, unpleasant way with aggressive energies, but rather in a gentle, forgiving way of releasing, with a sense of "Farewell; have a nice life; I'm going on with my life now." This required Pirjo to realize that she has her issues, her partner has his, and that for everything in life there is a reason. All the relationships in our lives, be they personal or professional, are relationships we need at a given time. It is therefore important to get to the bottom of these relationships, clear any issues or conflicts that may arise, and learn our lessons from them. It is important to remember that these relationships are merely mirrors of our self—they are not about other people, but about us.

Once a relationship is no longer intertwined it becomes easier for both parties to move on. During the second session with Pirjo, we worked with Holographic Repatterning, gradually shifting her consciousness from sadness into acceptance and peacefulness. Aside from maintaining forgiveness and peace, the process also allowed Pirjo to open up and invite in a new relationship that would be happier and healthier. In the next stage, we cleansed her home in order to avoid negative thought forms and energies from returning to her home, and to protect it from any anger or negative thoughts her former partner may have, which could affect her and her children.

Another aspect of my work involves energetically assisting in the transition of terminally ill individuals. I assist them in preparing to transition peacefully, as well as help prepare the ones who are left behind to let go. The session usually includes defining exactly how people will leave this world when they are ready, in physical terms. This allows both the patient and the family to understand exactly what to expect. It also allows them the relief of knowing that the person is dying in the way they had designed. Finally, it allows the patient to transition in peace and go with great dignity in their own time.

During the 1990s, I began learning and practicing remote viewing. Occasionally, the family of a murder victim, seeking help to solve the case, approaches me. I go "in," "look," and tell them what I see. What comes through is often very accurate and of valuable assistance to the police working on the case. If the case is cold, however, what I "see" often cannot be proven in a court of law because of a lack of hard, physical evidence. The most important part of the work is helping the family come to an acceptance of their loss and to a place of peace so that they can move on with life.

Aside from helping people to heal their souls and prompt the changes they want to see in their lives, I am also a storyteller. I enjoy reading my haunting tales of timeless love, mystery, and moral beauty aloud to spellbound audiences. The stories explore the dramatic theme of obstacles to love and derive from the collective unconscious. In each story, there is some reason why two lovers cannot be together. These are soul-mate love stories that help people explore archetypes in order to come to a place of tolerance, a place of live-and-let-live. Furthermore, I believe the stories reflect the Canadian acceptance of multi-culturalism, since they are set in different times, places, and cultures from all over the world.

It is important to remember that life sends us all challenges—we all experience bad days. In these cases, it is vital not to succumb to the stress but to learn to stay in your power! Whenever a new challenge comes along, we have the choice of reacting in the same old way we always have or trying a new way. A young woman who was miserable in her marriage once visited me. After listening to her dilemma, I told her that I could not tell her whether or not she should stay in her marriage. Instead, I asked her what would make her happy. Our happiness is the most important factor, and it is our fundamental right. I think that we all kick around in the third dimension until we find out what we do not want so that we can decide what we do want and then create it.

Helping to make a positive transformation in peoples' lives, however, requires more than just my expertise. First of all, I cannot work on someone unless they have given me permission to do so. Moreover, effective healing requires faith on the part of the client and a strong will to do what is necessary in order to facilitate the shift. They need to be ready to make the change. My favorite kind of client is the one who's doing her work. If you are upset about something for more than 20 seconds, it is your issue, and if you do not do the work to acknowledge and resolve it, it will only intensify over time. Therefore, I strongly believe that people who are continuously working on their issues are on the right track with their lives, working towards becoming a better person.

Often, I hear clients say, "I need to lose weight, quit smoking, find a job, and save my marriage. I need a miracle!" This miracle will happen only when they are ready and committed to accepting it. Some people need to meditate and fully understand the process and change, and therefore will take longer to be ready to change. Others can accept it immediately. Everyone is allowed to make her own miracle according to her own time line.

Another great benefit from my work is that I can do it on myself! If I wake up at three in the morning in a panic about something, I get up and do a session on myself, feeling the frequencies change within me. Also, each and every one of my clients brings me something I need to learn. The sessions always involve tremendous exchange. Many of the issues my clients approach me with are issues I may have had or am experiencing myself. I learn so much from them since it is easier to be an external, objective person looking into others' issues and seeing what needs to be done.

I once had a client who came up with a new idea of heaven and hell: All that happens when you die is you automatically go to heaven, where God hands you a video of your life, and you watch it over and over and over again. If you had a good life and did good things: helped others, made a difference, came to your own epiphanies and understandings, and were generally a good person, then watching the movie is heaven! If, on the other hand, you were a crumb, did not contribute to the world, caused other people pain, and generally made the world a lesser place because of who you were and what you did, then watching the movie is hell! Ever since I heard this interpretation, I get up every morning and say, "Okay, God, let's make it another good day on my video!" I would like to watch a good movie at the end of my journey, and through my work I get to help others create good movies as well.

I have been working with clients since 1984 and have been very satisfied in this line of work. I enjoy sharing my knowledge and experiences, and through this, giving back to the community. One of the greatest benefits of my work and the main thing that has kept me going all these years is the feedback I receive from my clients. There is no better feeling than to receive a call from a client several months after working with them and hear, "I haven't had a migraine for so long; thanks!" "I'm getting along so well with my little boy now," "My daughter got an A+ in math," or "My husband finally got a good job." It is wonderful when people see the connection with the work we do!

—Jeannie Mackay

You can learn more about Jeannie Mackay at: www.jeanniemackay.com

Al Molyneaux—Futurist, Trance Programmer, Corporate Lecturer, and Financial Strategist

Photo: Yanka Van der Kolk

I first heard of Al from a friend. Out of curiosity, I met with him and soon discovered the great benefits of working with him. Our conversations on both the spiritual and practical levels are always intriguing and informative, transcending into the extraordinary.

Al's input in my life is not limited to any one aspect or field, as it spans across both my business and personal life. In our work together we focused, for example, on the hiring of staff for my practice, the formulation of marketing strategies, the sale of my practice, and more. Al was the one who inspired me to write my first book—an idea that probably would not have occurred to me otherwise!

The main goal in my work with Al is to enhance my healing process by clearing and neutralizing my karma. This can be done by creating the right changes in my life, avoiding distractions, and moving forward in my path. With Al's support, I learned that I should not be afraid to question my life and to ask the right questions in order to get the answers I need. Throughout this process I am constantly searching for clues around me by exploring events, actions, words, and feelings in my daily life.

One of the methods Al and I use in our sessions, for example, is the exploration of my past lives. Revealing who I was and what relationships I had in past lifetimes has helped explain many aspects of my present life. Most importantly, it has assisted me in the process of healing both my present and previous lifetimes.

Listening to Al's stories is fascinating, and there is no end to the miracles that occur through our meetings. During the years we have worked together, he has given me a global perspective on the direction I should take to ensure success in everything that I do. He advised me on how to avoid the pitfalls of human nature and circumstance, and has helped me find the courage to pursue my dreams and goals. Gradually with Al's support, I have grown to trust myself.

—Pirjo Friedman

When I was seven years old, I fell nearly fifty feet from a tree and was knocked unconscious. When I came to, I remember wondering, "*What am I doing in this body?*" My body felt foreign to me, and my mother can testify that my interests and hobbies changed entirely overnight. I became a walk-in soul, where one soul vacates a body and a new soul enters. Apparently, my new soul had very powerful psychic abilities. That is how I found myself at the early age of seven possessing very strong electrical energy, and having the ability to read others' minds, pasts, and futures. My strong intuitive ability is manifested in my left hand—if someone is telling the truth or if they should be doing or acting on something, my left hand heats up. If the hand remains cold, I would advise them not to follow that path.

Many years afterwards, I received a visit from a German woman who was at one time Hitler's astrologer. She claimed that she had never felt energy as strong as that emanating from me. Although I always had a sense of its strength, her confirmation certainly explained the numerous electrical car problems I'd had in the past, why I tended to trigger the alarms in airports, and why I was always having to change the light bulbs around my house!

I discovered another indication of my psychic abilities several years ago when I went to see an ophthalmologist, who had no knowledge of me or what I do for a living. While examining my eyes he expressed great surprise, noting that I have three crosses in my inner eye. I was uncertain what this meant or why he seemed so interested. Excitedly, he explained that having crosses in one's inner eye was a sign that a person was extremely psychic. He was speechless when I finally confirmed my psychic abilities to him.

Although I was aware of my psychic abilities from an early age, my career path initially took an entirely different direction, as I worked for many years as the president of a company. In the early 1970s my brother and his wife passed away, leaving behind a 12 year-old, girl, Dawn Marie. My wife Frances, and I, who never had children of our own, took her in. We enrolled her at a public school, but soon discovered this was not working out. Frances and I knew my niece had great potential, and therefore, we transferred her to a private boarding school. Within three months she was the smartest kid in the school! One weekend Dawn Marie came home and said, "I have been telling the headmaster that you are the president of a company but that you also have psychic abilities." Apparently, she had volunteered my services for the school for two days in order to help raise money for orphans overseas. The teachers and other parents were so intrigued by my readings, that before I knew it they were all lined up down the hall, waiting to see me! This is how I began my career as a futurist. Following this experience I retired from the business world at the age of forty and was free to focus on my new and exciting path.

Over the years, my business grew based solely on word of mouth and personal referrals. My client list is long and diverse, spanning nearly all professions and occupations. I am often approached by corporation managers, lawyers, and doctors who seek my input as to gain perspective and advice, although some of them do not approach me directly. Roughly 80 percent of my clientele are women, and a substantial number of them are wives of the managers, lawyers, and doctors. For some reason my line of work seems to appeal more to women, perhaps since they are less intimidated by spirituality and the unknown.

I always took pleasure in talking with and counseling people, and my work allows me to do this in myriad ways. First, I enjoy reaching out and helping people by networking and connecting them with others that may assist them in some way. Networking is therefore a vital part of my professional and personal life. The main part of my work includes readings for people. Although some of my clients initially approach me with some reserve and skepticism, the feedback I receive from them is compelling! Not long ago I received an e-mail from a client who reminded me that in our meeting several years earlier, I had predicted that he will have great amounts of money, but that he should be aware of a Spanish-speaking lady and not marry her. He continued to inform me that he indeed became very rich as the owner of several shopping malls. He had however, married a Spanish-speaking woman, divorced her, and as a result, lost most of his assets!

Another time, a woman showed me a picture of her son, a handsome 21-year-old university football player. She inquired whether he was healthy, and I replied that he was not. Although there was no sign for concern, I urged her to take him to a neurologist as soon as possible. The son was seen by a neurologist, underwent all the tests, and was diagnosed as healthy. But I was convinced that the woman should seek a second opinion. When she did, she called me back to express her gratitude. Her son was in the early stages of Hodgkin's disease, but fortunately, his condition was diagnosed in time.

Another time a client who was concerned about her health approached me. I assured her that she was perfectly healthy—she did not have a medical problem, but rather a guardian angel! Although I could not describe what the angel looked like, I could tell the woman that the angel comes to her bed every night and places a hand on her forehead, releasing intense heat. This surprised the woman. She said that indeed she had felt the heat on her forehead every night, and therefore thought she had a medical problem. She had even gone to see a neurologist! Throughout her session, we confirmed that the hand belonged to her late mother, her guardian angel.

During the 1980s I received a visit from a client who was concerned about global events and the risk of war. During our session, I forecast that a major new currency would be created in Europe, and that a week after this currency began circulation in American banks, somebody would commandeer American airplanes and fly them into the World Trade Centre, causing the buildings to collapse. I also forecast that a major portion of the Pentagon would be destroyed during the same event. As it happened, the Euro went into circulation in the United States in August 2001; the tragedy of the Twin Towers occurred in September of that year.

A method I often use with my clients during our sessions is hypnotherapy, which is one of the greatest tools we can use to connect to the subconscious mind, our powerhouse. Hypnosis can be used to alleviate all sorts of conditions, such as phobias and speech impediments. It is incredible what you can achieve through hypnotherapy! During a hypnotic session I am able to relax the client's body and mind to the point that the body and subconscious begin to open up. When this happens, we can begin to explore the subconscious, removing any blockages that might be there. Once these blockages have been opened up or removed, everything starts to flow smoothly. The change is immediate.

During hypnosis I often program post-hypnotic suggestions. These specify an action that is to be performed by the hypnotized person following the session in response to a cue or when encountering a certain situation. The suggestion can be easily changed, and can be pretty much anything: a mental, psychological, or physical note, such as touching one's ear or chin. When I was young, for example, I had a terrible fear of public speaking. After being hypnotized that all changed! During my hypnosis, the professor installed a post-hypnotic suggestion: that I touch my chin whenever I become nervous about presenting or lecturing. Since that day I have been more articulate and focused on whatever I was doing, and often when I appear on television, I am asked: "Al, you touch your chin an awful lot. Is that an idiosyncrasy?"

Some of my clients who are movie stars are nervous about receiving an Academy Award, no matter how charismatic and confident they are when they act. Standing on stage with no role or character to hide behind makes them nervous. Many times at home, Frances would rush me to the television saying, "There is so-and-so touching her ear, her diamond earrings, with the post hypnotic suggestion you gave her to boost her confidence!"

Hypnotherapy is also a very effective method to find out about our past lives—an important aspect of one's healing process. Many of us are fascinated with certain things that we cannot explain. Many times we may see a person and think, "*I know that person from somewhere, somehow.*" This phenomena can easily be explained by examining our past lives, which are recorded in our sub-conscious. Our interests may be derived from our past lives. For example, Pirjo's daughter, Tamar, has a great interest in swords, archery, and horses, for no apparent reason. Perhaps she used to be a knight in her past life.

Familiar people are ones we may have encountered in previous lives, and whom we are drawing once again into our energy fields for some reason. I, for example, was King Henry VIII in one of my past lives. In my hypnosis I saw myself holding a quill pen, signing the orders for executions of people. In another life I was giving orders on a boat, wearing tight pants with a sword at my side. I was a pirate, judging by the flag of my ship. That sure explains my own fascination with swords!

In our work together, Pirjo and I explored her past lives as well, which I think has explained a lot about her as a person and her ambitions in life. I believe that Pirjo has been a care giver for many lifetimes, which explains her strong desire to help others, either by pursuing her medical career or by networking and bringing the right people together.

One of my friends is a concert pianist, and was telling me about a little boy who already, at the age of seven, is performing professionally. My friend is in his forties and has spent a lifetime practicing to become a professional pianist, while along comes this little boy who appears to have just been born with it. The boy's hands are not even large enough for the keyboard, and yet he plays magnificently! I explained to my friend that the boy was probably a pianist in a past life, so he only needed to uncover the skill from his subconscious. The connection with past lives is so powerful that it can transcend even physical limitations such as the boy's small hands!

I once informed one of my clients that he had been a general from the South in the Civil War, and predicted that one day he would find his grave as well as a picture of himself. Several years later, this gentleman traveled to New Orleans and joined a tour of the city. During the tour, the group visited an old building, and as people were coming out of it, they were all staring at him. When he asked them if anything was wrong, they told him, "Yes, your painting is hanging above the fireplace!" It turned out that the picture inside was of a general, who was indeed identical to him! The gentleman then drove to the graveyard, looking for the general's tombstone, but could not find it. When he returned to his car, however, he noticed that he was parked right next to the general's grave!

Learning about our past lives is important to the healing of both this life and our past lifetimes since it channels energy from our previous paths into our lives today. By healing oneself fully, you have the potential to draw enough energy from the universe to affect healing globally. It is also important to know who you were in your past lives since we are prone to repeat the same patterns and mistakes in each life time, creating a negative karma which will require mending in the next life, if only we'd remember....

Changing your life story or your fate can therefore be achieved simply by realizing that you are repeating your own patterns from previous lives and by consciously deciding to make the change in your present life. For this, people need to uncover who they were in their past lives and what patterns and mistakes they tend to repeat. With this knowledge I believe anyone can change his or her fate.

I believe the most important part of healing oneself is truly believing in God, in your guardian angels, and in yourself. To this day, whenever I need to give a presentation or a lecture, for example, I turn to God, asking him to take over my brain, help me do a good job, and impress all the intellectuals in the crowd. Once I was particularly nervous before a lecture, as I was lecturing to over two thousand people. In my little pep talk with God beforehand I said: "If I do a good job tonight, would you let three people come up and congratulate me?" My lecture was supposed to end at 9:30 p.m. Although the lecture hall was not very far from my home, I only got back to my residence at one in the morning. The whole audience lined up to see me and congratulate me! Today I do not get as nervous before lectures as I did before, but I still pray for God's help before each one. I learned my lesson when prior to one presentation I had the audacity to say, "God, I don't need you tonight. I am feeling confident, and I can do a great job. I would like you to take the evening off and enjoy yourself!" That night I bombed. Needless to say, I have never repeated that mistake again!

One night I was driving my brand-new car and decided to take a shortcut over a small country road. At some point, however, while driving up a hill, I hit some black ice on the gravel road and completely lost control of my car. I was spiraling down the embankment, and was heading straight into a cement hydro tower below. I was sure I was going to die, but could not think of anything else to do but yell out, "God, help me!" At that point, it was as though a hand had come down and slapped the side of the car, pushing it out of its path towards the cement tower. At first I was very calm, but soon afterwards I started shaking, thinking about the miracle I had witnessed. How on earth was I still alive? But I knew. I trusted in God's ability to help me, and he came through.

Several years ago I was visiting in Florida and had a massive heart attack. Five cardiologists examined me and they all agreed—I did not have long to live. To this I said, "I am not going to die. I know the head surgeon here." Since I was from Canada, the doctors inquired of his name and how I knew the head surgeon. "God," I replied. "Dr. God. He will save my life." A quadruple bi-pass was called for, and before my surgery the doctors advised me to say goodbye to my wife, since they thought the damage to the lower valves of my heart was too extensive, and the risk of the operation high. As I was wheeled into the operating room, I asked my wife, who has tremendous healing ability, to place her hand over my heart. I had faith that through her hand, God would repair and heal my heart. All during the medical procedure, the doctors were puzzled—they could no longer find the damage! When they brought me down from the operating room the nurses told my wife that they had never seen such a beautiful heart.

I believe that everybody has psychic abilities, though they may call it intuition, a hunch, or gut feeling. This is why when we meet a person, we either like or trust them or we don't. We can tell if they are intelligent or pleasant, and we know these things almost immediately. Therefore, I do not believe I can do something other people cannot. I only have more practice than most.

One of the main reasons I continue doing what I do is the fabulous feedback I receive from my clients. There is no greater feeling in the world than receiving a call from the manager of a large corporation saying "Al, we did exactly what you advised us, and we are really starting to make money now. We are doing so much better!"

I once had a meeting with a man who was nervous about the reading. When I told him he was going to blow up in three months, he got up to leave, saying that I was scaring him and that he should not have come to me in the first place. I reassured him that by having this information, he could save his own life. The man asked where this would supposedly happen, and I mentioned a small luxury boat. I could see the boat exploding; his body in the air, and his flailing arms on fire. As it happened, this man had an antique boat, which he had been restoring. I advised him he was doing something wrong on the dashboard. Three months later, nearly to the day, the boat blew up. The man returned to me several months later with bandaged arms and said, "I put the key in the ignition of the boat, and as I turned it I saw your face. Immediately I covered my own face with my hands, and the gasoline went down my arms, burning them, and that was the last thing I remember until I hit the water." A bolt off the dashboard had shot into his hand. If he had not covered his face, it would have gone through his eye and into his brain, and would have killed him immediately. "You saved my life," he continued. "Why did I not listen to you?"

This skepticism is something I encounter every day. Most people, even those who have gone to see psychics in the past, think of them as kooks or crooks, and take everything we say with a grain of salt. Imagine the possibilities of healthier, happier lives if people let go of that fear, and simply listen.

—*Al Molyneaux*

You can learn more about Al Molyneaux at: www.executivecorporateedge.com

Liz Nash—Senior Creative Director

Since Liz and I first met through the Women Entrepreneurs of Canada organization several years ago, we have come together in numerous other networking meetings and events. Over the years, I discovered that Liz has a special ability to pick up on the needs of others and creatively address them in various ways. Therefore, aside from being good friends, I have used Liz's expertise for designing and creating the promotional material for my business.

During our work together, Liz explained to me the importance of delivering the right message to my existing and potential customers through promotional materials. Furthermore, she explained that it is equally important to be true to my own tastes, so long as they do not deter customers. This achieves continuity in delivering the message, whether it is through the internal design of the place, the attitude of the staff, or the promotional material itself, such as the business cards and the websites.

To begin our work, Liz came to my practice in order to get a feel for the place and its environment. Since the interior design was already complete, we used it to set the tone for the marketing materials Liz later developed. Next, Liz asked me to come up with words that I felt described the practice. These words helped to define the identity and image of the business. I felt that this exercise was crucial in order to base the marketing material on the atmosphere and identity that the clinic had already developed over the years. For example, I have never been attracted to the humorous advertising so often used in dentistry; involving comical figures with huge teeth and gigantic toothbrushes. Rather, I strove to achieve a more tasteful image that conveyed a caring, soothing and healing environment that supports you before, during, and after your treatment. This same environment is communicated by the design and setup of my practice.

In the future, as I develop my new business, I look forward to working with Liz again. This time, as opposed to our work on the practice, we will start from scratch to create a brand new business identity and image. I am excited to see how this process will interlink with the work of other members of my team. For example, while Marcelene and I create the vision statement for the new business, Liz and I will build a new identity, design, and marketing strategy deriving from this vision.

—Pirjo Friedman

My career started when I studied design and advertising at the Ontario College of Art and Design in Toronto, Canada. During my studies I met Rod, my husband, who was a designer and art director himself. Rod had studied in Australia and moved to Toronto because he was attracted to the field of corporate identity—a field that at the time was burgeoning and gaining importance in North America.

Once I graduated I got my first job as an art director at a large agency in the city. Soon after, Rod became a creative director in a new agency that he helped open in Toronto after working in their Buffalo, New York, office. Rod, however, had always dreamed about us opening our own business and working together. In Australia he often observed couples working closely together and noted that the working relationship was very intense and the resultant synergies immense, especially in our industry where one is always drawing on infinite creativity. It is not unusual for spouses to become jealous of such a relationship, and so Rod believed it would be handier and more exciting if we worked together.

In 1972 we were finally ready to realize our dream and open our own business. We started with people who knew our previous work, and we gradually won some large clients. When their executives moved on to work with other companies, they called us to work on their marketing communications and corporate identity. The identity may have been an existing image that merely needed an upgrade; it may have involved creating a new name following a takeover or a merger; or it required the creation of a new identity for a brand new company. Through our vast and diverse experience, we became very adept and experienced at creating and managing corporate identities and branding.

Many people associate identity with a company's logo, which appears on their letterhead, business cards, brochures, and website, but that is only part of a company's identity. Corporate identity and brand include the physical plant, buildings, and location of the company; the way they greet their customers; their human resources ideologies; and the corporate culture cultivated by the company. Furthermore, it includes any marketing and promotional strategies and activities, and any other way in which the company conveys its identity and image to existing and potential customers, investors, bankers, suppliers, or employees. Practically everything about the business constitutes its identity and brand, including how the company is going to be run, what and how they are selling, who will be working there, and the target market.

In the process of upgrading a corporate identity for an existing company, we often collect all relevant information and material about the company in what we refer to as a "communications audit." It is important to know what the company already has, since as we create or develop the identity, everything related to the business must be considered and aligned in order to convey a consistent message. For example, during our work with a major downtown hotel, the audit located hundreds of items carrying the hotel's logo: the dining room, lounge, café, room service, and restaurant menus, matchbooks, towels, laundry bags, bathroom amenities, billing stationery, paperwork, and so forth. During our work with Pirjo, she started her own audit as well, collecting her stationery, paperwork, manuals, notices, newsletters, business cards, and so on. We often advise clients conducting an audit to spread out all the collected material on a table and then ask themselves, "Do these look like they all came from the same company? Do they make my company look as good as it really is?"

Another useful method is for clients to brainstorm a list of words which they associate with their business and its character. Many people are more comfortable working with words than with visual material. They may choose words or phrases such as: responsive, service oriented, leading edge, pushing the envelope, or utilizing high-tech scientists. The words may indicate the company's type of business, target market, long-term goals, vision, or values.

Eventually, through compiling such a list, clues to the style and character of the company appear, and we can start transforming those clues into their new image or brand. During our work with Pirjo, for example, she provided us with good direction by describing her business with words such as: nurturing, positive energy, respect, dignity, helping the community and networking. We visited the clinic to get a further feel for the atmosphere and the people. Lastly, we compared the identity of the clinic that was shaping through our research with the identity conveyed in the promotional material that had been done in the past.

When some managers take office they feel the need to change the corporate image as to put their own personal "stamp" on the company. Others may wish to create a new identity for their company because they are tired of the way it looks. Changing an existing identity, however, should be done only in certain circumstances and with good reason, for example, if your current image is failing or hurting the company, or if it does not portray who you are. It is important to remember that corporate identity has equity and value. Therefore, when we are asked to change an existing identity, we suggest to maintain as much continuity as possible between the old and the new images, retaining as much of the equity as possible, while trying to make the changes effective enough to achieve the goals. We once worked with a technical company in the pulp and paper industry that had quite a dreadful logo that was completely unrelated to their business. In surveys of which ads were noted and read in a leading industry magazine, their ads scored last; therefore they did not have much equity to lose to begin with. Rod and I created a long-term plan and changed their image to that of a highly technical company. The new ad campaign was so successful it boosted their recognition from the bottom of the pile to become the second- or third-most-recognized company in the industry! This change was achieved mainly through identity modifications and changes in the advertising and promotions that reflected the new image.

When dealing with a new company where there is no previous material on which to base a communications audit, the method we often use is termed "benchmarking," and it involves an examination of other companies—the communications commonly used by the competition. This process helps us to more fully understand the playing field. For instance, customers in a certain industry may be used to seeing very basic printed material. Another industry, however, may have set the bar higher, with costly brochures on luxurious paper, or websites with extremely sophisticated interactive components.

Our work is most valuable when it is closely linked with strategic planning. We have created a "communications blueprint"—a single sheet of paper with four columns that has become a valuable tool in our work. The first column outlines the vision statement and objectives of the company. These may be to generate a certain amount of revenue, to give back to the community, to sell the company in five years, or to take advantage of a certain bubble in the market. The second column specifies the strategies created by the company with the purpose of achieving their goals. In the third column we list all existing and available communications that may be used to support the strategies outlined in the second column. The fourth and last column, which we often refer to as the "reality column," includes what can realistically be done and assigned to this year's budget. The tasks are prioritized, and budget figures are assigned to each item. While some tasks may not be performed for a while, it is valuable to be able to see the whole picture. For instance, if you are planning to create a website in the near future, then you will only require low-resolution photographs. If you know, however, that you are planning to design a brochure six months from now, you can ensure that the photos will be of sufficient resolution as to serve the brochure as well.

The communications blueprint encompasses the findings from the research and orientation. It lists the communication choices, and starts a plan of action outlined in the fourth column. Once the initial research of what the business is about has been done, our role is to use this research in designing the corporate identity. Our work involves working with colors, patterns, fonts and proportions, and the challenge is often to deal with other people's preferences and tastes. We may be the ones responsible for the design, but the owners and managers of the businesses will need to live and work with it. For this reason, it is essential that we comprehend our clients' tastes, consider their ideas and include these in the process.

Some people are not comfortable describing what designs they like, or they may feel that it is our job to decide on these things for them. Others, however, have strong, set ideas. For example, when we started working with Pirjo, she was very clear about what she believed was not right for her: the humorous, cartoon-type approach for logos and promotions. We continued to consult with her regarding her color, pattern, font, and proportion preferences, and she explained the significance behind the colors she had chosen for her business cards in the past and gave us samples of other colors that held specific meaning for her. Today, all of the clinic's promotional material and every aspect of the clinic's design is representative of Pirjo's vision, while clearly maintaining continuity with designs previously used in the clinic.

The designing of a corporate identity is manifested in myriad ways, such as logos, brochures, advertising materials, office design, and so forth. Business cards are often deemed very important, as they often form the first impression of a company. Cards are also powerful in the way they can lift employees, motivate them, and keep them excited about the business. In a corporate setting, however, this often needs to be carefully controlled. Once we were approached by an executive of a large corporation who was fed up with arguing with the other executives over how their business cards looked. The executives were free to design their own cards, each trying to look more important than the others, and none looking as though they belonged to the same company! Rod and I managed to get the situation under control by creating an identity manual for them that included a section specifically covering the business cards in a way that was accepted by all parties.

Another crucial aspect of business communications, particularly in today's Internet age, is the company's website. Today, many clients, customers, and patients choose one business over another, without ever having set foot inside the company's office, simply by judging the websites based on design, content, and whether their needs were met. Some companies rely on their websites for more than information provision, as they can also be used for booking, purchasing, and so forth. A few years ago, many sites sported elaborate "flash" animations. This novelty is wearing off, however, and people today are more attracted to simple, user-friendly sites that allow you to find what you are seeking quickly and easily. A recent trend in web-design is "Content Managed Sites" (CMS). These sites allow our clients to make daily changes on the site, without having to become computer experts. The design integrity of the site remains stable, while words and pictures can be added and taken away easily.

In our business, Rod and I offer a wide range of advertising and design services. I often describe our services as integrated or holistic marketing, where all the pieces work cohesively towards meeting the objectives. Our broad experience allows us to carefully build or enhance new brands with respect to the corporate culture, corporate image and the target audience.

—Liz Nash

You can learn more about Liz Nash at: www.nashnash.com

Jo-Anne Raynes—Financial Advisor

Photo: Yanka Van der Kolk

One of the greatest benefits I derive from my work with Jo-Anne is her advice and insight relating to my personal financial planning and portfolio management. Jo-Anne has helped me appreciate the importance of financial planning—of making financial decisions and commitments to support my future goals, especially now that I am planning to give up a regular business income with the selling of my practice.

As an entrepreneur, I create wealth not only for myself, but also for my employees. Being involved this way in other people's lives is exciting and satisfying. The financial well-being of employees, however, is largely dependent on how well the business is led and managed financially. This places a great amount of responsibility on the entrepreneur. One of the reasons I look forward to retiring and selling my practice is that it will release me from the heavy responsibilities of entrepreneurship. Salaries and expenses seem to accelerate over the years, requiring my constant focus on finding and retaining patients. I was happy to do this at one time, especially when it meant bringing additional benefits, such as the use of Reiki to my patients, but now I am ready for new challenges. My work with Jo-Anne has therefore focused on preparations for the sale of my practice and planning for my new business ventures.

In the past I would reinvest all of my earnings back into the business, focusing on the growth of the clinic. Based on my consultations with Jo-Anne, however, I decided that in future I would invest 20 percent of my capital in my new business ventures, and put the remaining 80 percent aside in an investment portfolio. I will be investing the portfolio in assets that can provide me with both a regular income stream and long-term capital growth, protecting me at least to some degree from inflation. Jo-Anne tells me that a dollar today will be worth only 67 cents in 20 years, assuming that inflation continues at its current rate of two percent annually. I have spent enough sleepless nights to last a lifetime! Taking such action and realizing my financial plan will enable me to experience less risk and stress.

While I have always managed the finances of my business responsibly by employing the services of professionals, I did not always pay deliberate attention to this in my personal life. For example, I never planned a structured saving or investment strategy for my children or myself, although I have set up several sporadic savings accounts for them (and completely forgotten about them for many years until the banks brought them back to my attention). I realize now that I may have missed some good opportunities to make better investments, save taxes, or pay my mortgages more quickly, saving considerable dollars in interest payments.

Over the years I have learned to take calculated risks and trust my intuition. One of the main investment opportunities I have capitalized on has been real estate. By purchasing real estate, renovating it and renting it, I was able to pay off my mortgages. The sale of these investments, sometimes bringing up to 30 percent appreciation in value, has not only enabled me to reinvest the capital but has enhanced my lifestyle over the years. I can barely believe that in the past year alone I sold more than a million dollars of real estate!

After I have worked with Marcelene on the overall goals of my business, and with Marlene on the strategies required to reach these goals, and the challenges I may face in the process, Jo-Anne and I explore the strategies required to reach these goals, outlining the challenges I

may face in the process. Jo-Anne's role is to examine these challenges and manage my finances accordingly, generating ideas as to how I can reach my goals from a financial point of view.
—Pirjo Friedman

Money is a source of power—the power to create the life you envision and generate positive change. Money also gives you the power to affect the lives of others. For example, your children can be educated, or your new ventures may enable strategic social change through charitable giving. And while we may not all be able to leave a substantial cash legacy, we can take out an insurance policy that will pay a sum to an organization we are passionate about.

Managing your overall investment portfolio goes beyond simply managing dollars. I always encourage clients to think of their investment portfolio as a business in and of itself. As a business, it requires your leadership, clarity, and attention, ensuring it is on the right track to meet your goals and taking you where you want to go: towards greater financial independence and choice in your life.

The simple process of pulling together all the details of your financial situation can be immensely clarifying and liberating. It can also identify new options. For instance, I often find business clients are unaware that they can have indexed pensions, much like their colleagues in corporate life.

I have always been attracted to the entrepreneurial process, a process that can be likened to sculpting the unknown, a form of art that brings new possibilities and connections into being. I feel privileged to have spent the majority of my career financing entrepreneurs and assisting in the growth of their businesses.

In my current role as a financial advisor and entrepreneur, as I build and grow my own practice, I encourage entrepreneurs such as Pirjo to look at their businesses as one of the assets (albeit a large one) in their personal investment portfolio. This asset can be reinvested in and grown, or sold at some point, much like other assets in one's portfolio. This framework can be very helpful in thinking through decisions such as whether to continue a business in its current form, move onto other interesting ventures, or retire, for example.

The first step in running a business and managing your finances is the setting of goals. Goals are shorthand for saying, "This is what I want to be doing, what I want to accomplish." Clarifying our goals may sound a tad daunting, but keep in mind that business and financial goals are not cast in stone. Goals change as we change and as our vision of the future opens up. Without these goals, however, we will not get to first base, let alone realize our destiny and manifest who we are.

Sometimes we may only have an inkling of what we want to do, or have forgotten our desires. For example, a friend of mine built an advertising agency from scratch, sold it, and moved on to build a thriving consulting practice. One day he found himself at a stage where consulting no longer interested him as it did in the past, and he no longer knew what he wanted to do. When we met I asked him, "Well, what did you really want to do when you were fourteen?" He said, "Actually, I always wanted to bind books!" When I phoned him a month later, he told me that after our meeting he had gone out and bought bookbinding equipment and materials. He followed his sense of destiny and started binding books. Today he thoroughly enjoys himself, rescuing historical books and other antiquities and making a further contribution to the world as a go-to expert. I believe that we all come into this world with attractions to certain things and a sense of what we are meant to be doing. When we manage the money and resources that come into our hands, we increase the possibility of being able to pursue our interests and desires as they reveal themselves to us.

Managing finances is essentially about risk management and protecting your investment portfolio and your business from losses. For instance, people tend to forget that they themselves are one of the key assets in their investment portfolio. Failing to protect their income and their businesses from loss through insurance can be costly. Sickness and disabilities can drain an investment portfolio and put the equity that has been built up in a business at risk. This can happen when a key person is no longer able to do her job and ongoing costs cannot be covered.

When Pirjo was consulting with me regarding her insurance coverage, we discussed whether or not she should invest in disability insurance for herself, and in business continuation insurance for her clinic. If she were operating her business alone, I would have advised her to do so. Pirjo, however, employs an experienced and competent team who are able to lead the business. Should something happen to her, the business would continue to operate regularly, enabling salaries and operating costs to be paid, and providing Pirjo with a basic income to get by. In this case, Pirjo decided to forgo disability insurance and business continuation insurance, alleviating some costs. Once Pirjo sells her business and will no longer enjoy a regular income, she will not be able to access disability insurance for herself. However, she may consider long-term care insurance in the event that she will require considerable care later on in her life.

The key when considering insurance is to fully understand the costs and benefits.

One of the main areas in which I advise my clients relates to retirement. What does retirement mean these days? We often use the word without much consideration, and as a consequence I believe we are limiting our possibilities. As an alternative I have begun using a new word: *regeneration*. Given that we have such a long and healthy life expectancy, I believe we are better served to think of this period of our lives in terms of new life challenges, of regeneration, in whatever appealing form this may take, such as financial and emotional commitments to new ventures. This is the process that Pirjo has been working through and making preparations for. Pirjo is at a point in her life where she has built a pool of capital and created options for herself. She has wisely considered how much of this capital she will devote to ensuring her peace of mind through a safety net that ensures her long-term well-being, and how much she will commit to new ventures that are a part of her regeneration plans. These ventures may have been dreams she has had in her life, or visions that have become clearer to her over the years.

The important thing when planning for retirement, or regeneration, is to save on a regular basis. Clients often do not realize the magic and power of compounding and how time can grow their savings. Take the wonderful mathematical rule of 72, for instance: State the rate of return you expect to earn over your investment horizon and divide it into 72. If it is 8 percent, for example, then according to this rule you will double your money in 9 years' time. The more you will save and invest, the more you will earn in 9 years time. This is a simple, helpful method of calculating how much you can accumulate over a period of time.

Growing and investing in a business is the essence of being an entrepreneur. To be successful, the business has to possess *you* and to be your top priority. It must consume your attention, leaving little time to pursue other interests. It requires that you put your team before yourself and assume most of the risks. All this works to increase the value of the business and creates the financial benefits of entrepreneurship. But it can become a burden as we find ourselves gently nudged to move on to new ventures.

When entrepreneurs decide to sell their businesses they may do so because they feel the time is right or because a buyer has entered the scene. Some however, like Pirjo, get to a point in their lives where they desire freedom from the constant preoccupation and focus on the business, and from the constant problem solving. Pirjo is now ready to sell. She has done well and achieved her goals; she has built a fine team that will continue to grow the business. Pirjo's efforts and innovations have benefitted many people, which is an accomplishment to be proud of. She understands now that the right way to move forward is to wrap up her involvement in the business and release herself from its possession, rather than continue to be engaged in it, even in a minor way. Only by letting it go will she allow for new opportunities to emerge and move her forward.

I would like to leave you with one final thought: Money has been described as congealed energy—it can be accumulated and spent wisely or not leveraged at all. It's up to you. Live forward and be good to yourself!

—Jo-Anne Raynes

You can learn more about Jo-Anne Raynes at: www.Jo-AnneRaynes.com

Snezana Tomic— Homeopath and Astrologer

Photo: Yanka Van der Kolk

Snezana and I both practice in the same building, one floor apart. Our physical proximity has allowed us to continuously and reciprocally refer clients to one another, thus benefitting both of our businesses extensively. Moreover, we have personally benefited from each other's knowledge and expertise—while Snezana is a patient at my practice, I often consult with her regarding astrology, homeopathy, and nutrition.

Snezana is both a homeopathic doctor and a European-trained medical doctor. She is also a talented astrologer—she reads my chart and advises me about the blueprint of my subconscious mind. To this day, the readings I have had with her have provided me with valuable insight into why I may be experiencing various universal pushes and nudges and how I should navigate my way through them. In the past, for example, we could see how my chart fit perfectly with my last relationship. My chart referred to self-esteem and self-worth issues that needed to be addressed. The poor state of my relationship and the timing of my decision to end it really fit in with these issues.

Another great benefit I derive from Snezana's astrology readings relates to my professional and personal relationships. Occasionally we would read the charts of family, colleagues, and friends, helping me to understand what others around me may be experiencing, to empathize with them, and at times even to help them out.

Aside from astrology, Snezana has helped me significantly as a nutritionist in alleviating the symptoms of menopause and other health problems. She has also assisted me in finding appropriate and effective homeopathic remedies for extreme emotional levels, thus supporting me through challenging periods. In my past, I would sometimes feel stuck in certain aspects of my life; resisting, yet trying to understand why things are not turning out the way I wished them to. I feel that these remedies have helped me flow more naturally through life.

Having Snezana as a friend and a member of my team has been a blessing. Working with her has enhanced my healing on both the physical and emotional levels. I feel more connected to myself and more flexible in dealing with change and circumstance. Snezana helped me realize that instead of fighting and resisting what the universe throws at me, I should simply flow and experience where it is trying to take me.

—Pirjo Friedman

Sitting in the waiting room of my practice one day, I was flipping through the pages of a magazine when an ad for holistic dentists caught my eye. Pirjo's picture in the ad jumped at me from the page and struck me—this was no ordinary dentist! When I looked at the address provided I was surprised to find that Pirjo's practice was in my own building! I immediately charged downstairs and introduced myself. Pirjo and I had an immediate connection, and from day one we experienced a natural flow and exchange of energy. Only two days after we first met, we had lunch together. I found myself telling her very personal things while thinking, "Why am I telling all these things to a perfect stranger?"

My relationship with Pirjo is invaluable. I feel connected to her and fortunate that I can easily meet and talk with her. Over the years, Pirjo and I have referred numerous patients to one another, as well as introduced each other to practitioners and other professionals. When I first opened my practice in 1996, I spent a lot of time and energy introducing myself to people in my building and trying to promote my practice and services, although I was never comfortable with the selling-myself approach. When I met Pirjo, I soon discovered that she was a master networker. It is from her that I learned how to connect and communicate with others with greater ease. I started to enjoy the process of meeting new people, as I was no longer preoccupied with how they might perceive me.

Homeopathy is a holistic system of medicine that enhances our own vital force, the doctor within us, by taking into consideration all aspects of the person: mental, emotional, and physical. Although various medical and herbal modalities can be used to heal health problems, homeopathy is a unique medicine since it can heal the physical aspect as well as the mental and emotional aspects—and all this with a single remedy!

Homeopathic remedies are chosen based on the totality of the mental, emotional, and physical symptoms the person is experiencing. They are created from natural ingredients such as herbal, mineral or vegetable substances diluted to the point where only a vibration of that substance remains. This vibration resonates with our own vibration, or vital force, healing us on an energetic level and therefore affecting us simultaneously on all levels. Changing one's mental and emotional state will lead to manifestation of an improved reality for that person. It is not the situation that changes when taking the remedy, but rather, our outlook on the situation. We will no longer view the situation as a threat and react to it, but rather, we will deal with it from a more positive, centered perspective. With Pirjo, for example, aside from dealing with menopausal changes in her body, I also prescribed homeopathic remedies aimed at supporting her whenever she was faced with mental or emotional situations that have challenged her in the past. The remedies did not "fix" these situations, but they enabled Pirjo to deal with them in a positive and effective way.

All businesses strive for repeat business. However, in health professions such as Pirjo's and mine we face a *Catch-22*: our business depends on patients having problems. If we are professional and alleviate these problems—patients are happy, but do not need to return. On the other hand, if the service is lacking, the patient will need further treatment, but is likely to take their business elsewhere. I believe that in the future, people will appreciate health practitioners that are geared towards preventative treatment. Though these businesses may not have as much repeat business, they will grow through personal recommendations and referrals of satisfied patients. This is the vision of my practice, and due to its preventative role, nutrition is an important aspect of my work.

I truly believe that most diseases stem as a result of an unbalanced diet and could therefore be prevented by adhering to a proper, healthy diet. Too much unhealthy, processed food will keep our energy down, thus limiting our efforts to improve our life and ourselves. Poisoning the body will cloud and clutter our awareness, affecting not only our body and mind, but our spiritual self as well. In my experience, I can give patients a remedy to boost their immune systems, but the remedy will never work to its full potential if they are eating incorrectly. Removing from our diet the foods that suppress our immune system is, therefore, vital for the success and enhancement of the homeopathic remedies.

Even people who do keep to a balanced diet may be at risk. The soil in North America is depleted of nutrients due to overuse of pesticides and insecticides that are destroying the natural balance of the minerals, such as zinc, selenium, and chromium in the soil. If the soil lacks the nutrients, the body will lack them as well. Therefore, even if you do eat fruits and vegetables, if they are not organic, you are ingesting the pesticides, not the nutrients. Since many of us are literally starved of nutrients, it is only a matter of time until disease sets in.

When I advise people regarding nutrition, I remind them not to think of fresh fruits and vegetables only in terms of the vitamins they contain, but to remember the vital force within them. When we eat raw foods, we are serving our body not only with the nutrients but also with the life force that immediately nourishes us on all levels. Furthermore, I recommend consuming whole food supplements rather than the isolated vitamins and minerals. A few years ago, I found an excellent product that contains a number of different fruits, vegetables and grains. I recommend this product to all my clients, since it is as close to raw fruits and vegetables as possible.

In my work I often use a bio-energetic testing device that measures electromagnetic changes in the body and signals any type of stressful reaction that the body experiences when a certain food enters it. This device is valuable in discovering food allergies and sensitivities that people may not be aware of and which contribute to the suppression of the immune system, thus resulting in health problems such as asthma, frequent colds, headaches, and hyperactivity in kids. A computerized machine stores the electromagnetic frequencies of all foods, since every food has a unique electromagnetic code. When applying the electromagnetic frequencies to the skin, the conductivity of the skin changes immediately, and the reading shows the body's reaction to a food, whether it accepts it or not. The device is more accurate and reliable than an allergy test, as the latter only measures whether the consumption of certain foods leads to the release of histamine in the body. If histamine is released, it means the body is positively allergic to that food. Food, however, can affect the body in many ways by interacting with the digestive and immune systems, or through various other mechanisms that may not involve the release of histamine. These can cause myriad reactions, such as drops in energy levels, mood changes, bloating and post nasal drip, to name a few.

Aside from practicing classical homeopathy and nutrition I practice astrology and the analysis of astrological charts. Though many people think of astrology as a predictive tool, the value of astrology lies elsewhere. An astrological chart is essentially a map, a blueprint of one's subconscious mind. It is important to understand this blueprint since the subconscious mind can manifest and attract certain people, situations, and circumstances that are the mirror images of our subconscious patterns, creating our reality. We are responsible for creating our own destiny. Astrology can also be used to shed light on the dynamics of the relationships that we have with others. By understanding what others may be going through in their lives, we can become more tolerant, patient, and compassionate towards them.

The planets used in astro-analysis are all associated with certain aspects of our lives. Understanding their movements and the relationships between them is an important part of astrology since it can be used as a tool for personal growth. For example, Saturn, the planet associated with responsibility, maturity, and soul searching, sends us challenges whenever it appears in our sign. It urges us to question our lives, be honest with ourselves, and face our fears. Furthermore, it drives us to deal with the obsolete in our lives, to give up anything blocking our progress or that is no longer serving us, be it our life style, work, or relationships.

To balance these challenging times, Jupiter, the planet of good luck, fortune, and expansion, sends us optimistic periods. We gain a more positive outlook on life, which in turn creates a more positive and prosperous reality. Jupiter is also associated with spirituality, divinity, and divine creation. During these periods we are awarded with the opportunity to act Godlike; easily manifesting and creating anything that we desire and believe will make us, and others, happy.

Pirjo and I meet regularly around her birthday to analyze her chart and see the dynamics she is undergoing at that time in her life. During one of our meetings I observed a challenging aspect in her chart between two planets: Mars and Neptune. Mars is a planet associated with self-expression and work. In women's charts it symbolizes the opposite sex, representing our partner, lover, or husband. Neptune, on the other hand, is a planet associated with our hopes and dreams, spirituality, and soul searching, and it also indicates blind spots, deception, and confusion in our life. This aspect of Neptune usually brings with it times of dissatisfaction and a loss of interest in one's work or certain aspects of it, as well as an increased desire to find one's true calling and purpose in life. In a relationship it can cause periods of disappointment that are brought on by a desire for a deeper connection, by unrealistic expectations, and by a tendency to self-deceive during our search for a soul mate.

Pirjo was experiencing these forces set forth by Mars and Neptune. She felt dissatisfied with her work and contemplated leaving her nine-to-five job and selling her practice. This was a major, life-changing decision. What we saw in her chart, however, helped her understand her feelings better. The chart confirmed that these urges were real and reassured her that she was on the right track by addressing them. Mars and Neptune also focused Pirjo's attention on her relationship, which was suffering at that time. She felt dissatisfied and realized that she was unhappy with the relationship—she wanted more out of it but did not get it. The planet's effect was analogous to taking off rose-colored glasses, thus helping Pirjo see the truth. Even though it was hard for her, Pirjo decided to stop fooling herself and to end the relationship.

Everyone encounters challenges in her life. Instead of resisting them, however, we should embrace these challenges. By embracing and facing them we will be able to achieve our biggest strides forward. By recognizing them as they arise, we can begin to see why they are happening and what we need to learn from them, and only then can we proceed to move forward in our lives.

—*Snezana Tomic*

Amber Valentyne—Yoga Instructor

I have been practicing yoga with Amber for several years, and our sessions are something I always look forward to. Amber has taught me both privately at my home and as a part of a group, such as at the Women Entrepreneurs of Canada organization board meetings. Amber is always flexible in her teaching and is enthusiastic when I spontaneously invite others to participate in our sessions—family, friends, and colleagues. Throughout the years, our personal interaction during the sessions has evolved into a strong friendship, as we enjoy sharing our experiences and knowledge with each other on a myriad of topics.

Over the years, yoga has become a vital part of my life. I cannot begin to describe the impact it has had on my health and particularly on my ability to remain flexible after many years of working in awkward angles at the dentist chair. Many years of work have resulted in various pains and aches in my body, which I had previously numbed with painkillers. Combining physical exercise and yoga, however, have helped me eradicate these pains completely.

Aside from improving my physical health, I discovered that yoga has a wonderful effect on other aspects of my life as well. For example, intuition is developed through our physical being as we learn to listen to our body's needs and responses. Therefore, it is crucial to learn how to tune in to our body, and yoga is an excellent tool for this. My yoga sessions with Amber promote my feelings of relaxation, the release of my worries, and the renewal and recharging of myself. In a nutshell, practicing yoga makes me feel younger and better!

During our sessions, Amber has taught me several stretching and breathing exercises that I can use anytime and anywhere, and which I have often used at the clinic. For example, whenever I administer local anesthetics to patients, I often guide them through deep breathing exercises—otherwise they would stop breathing, tense up, and increase their pain. The same is true for patients experiencing any other form of anxiety, or in fact, for any other life situation!

Amber has also introduced me to stability balls, which have made a great change in my life. Since the first time she brought them into my home, I have been using them while doing paperwork or sitting through long meetings. I soon discovered that the balls are a simple and practical answer to my pain—reducing the stress and impact on my back. And most of all—they're fun!

Amber's story of how she got to where she is today is a fascinating one. I admire the spirit, courage, and determination that are continuous in her history, and her strong belief in her profession. No doubt about it, Amber has converted me into a true yoga believer, to the point that practicing yoga is as natural to me as brushing my teeth!

—Pirjo Friedman

I was first introduced to yoga at the Kripala Yoga Center, which was originally established in Pennsylvania and has since moved to Lenox, Massachusetts. Over the years I learned from many talented teachers at the center, some being internationally renowned. I was the center's first advanced yoga teacher in Canada, and continued my studies in ashtanga, hatha, vinyasa, pre and post-natal, restorative, pranassage, yogassage and contact yoga. Over the years, my interests have expanded to other areas as well, such as massage, Reiki, and hypnosis.

When I first started teaching yoga twenty years ago, I was a "closet teacher"—an insurance broker sneaking out during lunch breaks in my business suit, with a leotard tucked away in my briefcase. During those days, practicing yoga was uncommon, almost secretive. Furthermore, coming from a family that valued success in the more traditional sense, I was forced to lead a somewhat double life. I therefore set up a small yoga program at a nearby neighborhood church and taught voluntarily to people living with AIDS.

After about two years of sneaking around teaching yoga, two of my friends committed suicide in a period of two weeks. The shock over these events led me to decide to make some changes in my life. I started teaching yoga more often, although still in a secretive manner, mainly out of concern for my family living in Hungary. At that time, before the fall of Communism in Hungary, yoga was considered illegal. During my trips there, my grandfather would often wince at the sight of my yoga books, warning me that getting caught would result in imprisonment. Naturally, this made me even more guarded and secretive about my passion and teaching.

In 1991 my daughter Jasmine was born. The period after her birth was a difficult one, as I experienced post-partum depression and was divorced soon after. My life became challenging and discontenting—there I was, with a child, working hard to pay my mortgages and trying to fulfill other peoples' desires and expectations of me. I had zero self esteem. It was through my yoga practice that I came to know myself and to heal my depression. In 1994 I finally decided to take control of my life and make some drastic changes—I finally closed down my insurance business and dedicated myself to what I wanted to do most—yoga.

In 1999, after living in the United States for several years, I returned to Canada and established the pre- and post-natal program at an existing yoga studio. Soon I discovered my love for working with pregnant women, accompanying them from start to finish, from pregnancy and labor through post partum. In 2003 I established the Twist Yoga Studio in Toronto, initially since I needed a new home for my pre and post-natal program. Essentially, I created a simple, sunny, and open space. In order to make it welcoming for everyone, I avoided cluttering it with strange objects, although I occasionally incorporate them in my own workouts. The studio offers a variety of classes such as: restorative yoga for people recovering from injuries; vigorous ashtanga classes which will make you sweat; and pre and post-natal sessions. Furthermore, we run a corporate program, offer massage therapy, shiatsu, and more. The studio includes a team of well-qualified teachers for all levels: if you have never done yoga before—great; if you have been doing it for years—wonderful! My ultimate goal is that after a session you feel enhanced and more attuned to your body, its movements, and how it should be treated in your day-to-day life. Listen to your body…notice how you feel.

Teaching yoga has been an exciting experience for me, and today I can reflect on how much I have evolved since the days I hid my yoga passion in my briefcase. Only after I committed myself fully to the profession, did I understand how being a successful teacher is not simply restricted to physically teaching the class. It is about finding a way of completely incorporating the yoga in life. My philosophy is that yoga is most valuable when practiced off of the mat. I feel that my work has been successful when someone starts to live and move differently, feeling better in their body and their life.

Today's society considers utilizing the body secondary to using the brain. As a result, most of us have the tendency to ignore our body, allowing it to become vulnerable to pain, aching and illness. This can be illustrated with our children most clearly—kids today do not move enough unless they are particularly athletic. They come home with hours of homework and spend the rest of the day watching television or chatting on MSN. Neighborhoods do not encourage them to go out and play unless they are involved in organized activities. Overall, kids are not moving enough, building up stress and tension in their bodies from an early age. Needless to say, most of us carry and accumulate this stress for the rest of our lives. Some of us may not even notice how much tension is trapped in our bodies until the physical and mental tension translate into pain, as they will when they are not released. The hips are a perfect example of this. In my teaching, I tend to concentrate on this area, since opening the hips does wonders to the releasing of compression in the lower back, the neck and the shoulders. Most people who do not practice yoga regularly do not notice their hips at all until they start moving them. When they finally do, however, a response I often hear is "Oh my goodness! I didn't notice how tight my hips were!"

Practicing yoga regularly can help us rediscover and reconnect with our bodies. It benefits us physically by keeping the muscles and joints open and limber. On an energetic level, it helps with the lymphatic drainage and circulation. Yoga can do wonders for promoting healing in some chronic health problems. For example, some of my older clients who have osteoporosis or arthritis often talk about having less pain as well as feeling taller and longer after their yoga sessions, since it releases some of the compression in the body. Another great benefit from yoga is maintaining a better posture, allowing you to stand, sit, and move around in a healthier way. Lastly, yoga promotes relaxation, as it opens and aligns the chakras. Yoga is not about standing on your head and making your body into a pretzel—it is about creative energy and opening the pathway of our body for that energy to flow.

The advantages of yoga, however, go well beyond the physical benefits. In my view, the most fascinating thing about experiencing yoga is interweaving it with all other aspects of life. Whether people realize it or not, yoga contributes to the expansion of the mind because it is a correlation of your mind and the movement of your body. Essentially, it is about conscious breath and conscious movement—getting in touch with how we feel within ourselves, and bringing us back to living in the present. One of my students once commented that her favorite thing about yoga is learning to "notice how you feel"—a phrase I often use in my classes. Noticing how you feel, without judgment or expectation—how your body feels, where does it feel differently from the way you want it to feel? Do you feel sad today? Anxious? Are you excited because your lover is coming home? If you don't like the way you feel, what can you do to change it? Most spiritual and religious practices refer to "being present," since the past is merely the story of where we have been and the future has yet to be created. By having that presence in your body you are inclined to become more intuitive and aware of your feelings, needs and desires, allowing you to make clearer decisions in your personal and business life.

For example, when you are hunched over your computer and your neck is tense, take notice of this, and take a few deep breaths and stretch. When you are feeling stressed, be aware that by changing your breathing pattern you can change your physiology as well as your psychology. People cannot breathe deeply when they are angry and tense, but as soon as they start breathing diaphragmatically, the body begins to unwind—and so does the mind.

A dental clinic is another example of this. Many people fear dentists and needles in general, leading them to a vicious circle: the stronger their fear, the more tension they create; the tenser they are, the more pain they experience. By coaching people how to breathe and relax, you can reduce levels of anxiety and tension, of pain, and gradually over time, of fear. This is, in fact, one of the elements differentiating Pirjo's dental clinic from others. I often hear people say, "Oh no, I have to go to the dentist!" But stepping into Pirjo's clinic is simply fun! Everyone's spirits are always high, and the atmosphere is energetic, though tranquil. In this atmosphere there is no place for tension or fear, especially with the staff's guidance on breathing and other relaxation techniques.

Certain emotions have physical locations in the body, though they may vary from person to person. Yoga can also be used as a means of releasing these emotions. For example, occasionally people will spontaneously and involuntarily begin to cry during a yoga class. While they are often startled by this reaction, I explain to them that it is simply the result of energy, which has been longing to be released for some time, being released from the body. Our belly is an example of this. The stomach is the body's center of power and unreleased emotion, as well as the center of our self-esteem—when we don't feel confident, attractive, empowered, or when we do not follow our gut; we get knots in our stomach. For this reason, I encourage people to roll on their stomach on top of the stability balls as to release any emotion captured in this area.

Yoga can contribute significantly to self-esteem as well. It enhances the understanding that the body is different on different days, and that every body is different. In my experience, anybody over the age of twelve feels challenged by certain aspects of yoga postures, whether backbends, forward bends, or inversions. To deal with these challenges, I emphasize throughout my teachings that yoga is about the process. It is not about whether or not you can perfect a posture that makes you feel better, but rather it is about the process of surrender—the realization that our bodies are limited on some days more so than others. We can guide it, encourage it, and treat it well, and remember that ultimately, we are not in control—not completely.

Although yoga contributes greatly to healing, I do not promote myself as a healer. The person doing the work is actually taking the journey—I am merely a guide, assisting with various tools and techniques. In my sessions, I like to start with "yogassage," or as one of my clients refer to it, "me doing the clients' yoga for them." As I do this, all of their weight is in my hands and I maneuver their body into various yoga positions. The client is in a relaxed state, and all they have to do is focus on their breathing. This also allows me to bring their body to a deeper level or stretch more quickly and safely. This also provides the opportunity for the client to experience some stretches that they can later use throughout their daily life. This method is effective, especially if my clients are very busy—despite their limited time frame they can still achieve significant results.

Another tool I use extensively is the stability ball. Stability balls can be used in a large variety of ways, from stretching, balancing, and strengthening the core, to just having fun. The best thing about the ball, however, is simply sitting on it! It is the habit of many of us to sit at work or at home, bending over, reaching for our keyboard, the phone or somebody's mouth if you are a dental hygienist. We sit with an inward rotation of the shoulders, compressed vertebrae in the neck and a lot of tension. In my experience, there is not one person on the planet that does not complain of neck or shoulder tension! Sitting on the ball while working on the computer, however, allows the spine to remain erect more naturally. Since you need to use your abs to stabilize yourself on the ball, whenever you start slouching you automatically, whether consciously or subconsciously, correct your position. Otherwise you will roll off the ball. The spine is a major energy pathway in the body that houses the central nervous system. Therefore, by sitting on the ball you not only develop your core strength, but you also feel more energized. Sitting on the ball also allows you to perform a few basic stretches: opening and releasing of the hips, stretching out the spine and chest, and so forth. This may take only two minutes, but in return you will achieve great energy flow. Many people tend to get droopy in the late afternoon and often reach out for chocolate, a muffin, or coffee for energy. While caffeine will stimulate circulation, this can be achieved more naturally on the ball, thus avoiding the interference of caffeine with your sleep later on.

Another exciting innovation I have recently completed is my newly released CD—"*Relax*." This is the second CD I have produced, and it includes a 30-minute guided relaxation, narrated by myself and accompanied by piano music in the background. I first created the CD after many years of making tapes for my clients geared to enhance their relaxation before falling asleep or as a means of recharging in the middle of the day. These tapes were very effective, since they allowed people to focus on the voice and music while quieting their minds from their everyday thoughts. The feedback I received was so positive that I decided to make a CD of professional quality.

Recently, I have expanded my practice to offer corporate programs as well. The purpose of these programs is to improve the health and output of employees. Although it is a recent development in the corporate world, many managers are realizing that offering yoga sessions to their staff will eventually improve their financial bottom lines. This makes sense, since when people feel better in their bodies and are not exhausted at their desks, they have fewer health issues, and they can, therefore think more clearly and work more efficiently.

In the past, Pirjo has taken advantage of this option as well. During the long Women Entrepreneurs of Canada board meetings, Pirjo invited me to lead a relaxation session that included stretching and breathing exercises. Although the session took no more than 25 minutes, the impact was significant! No matter how interesting the topic is, if you are sitting in a chair around a board table for hours on end, you get physically and mentally tired. By incorporating a relaxation session during the break, however, people can come back with renewed energy, a sparkle in their eye, better posture, and new ideas. If I had my way, every office and school would incorporate 15 minutes of yoga and relaxation a day!

Everybody can do yoga, at least to some degree. I have clients with multiple sclerosis who are bedridden, whom I literally stretch out because they cannot do it themselves. Some of my older clients have not sat on the floor in decades, let alone done yoga before, but today they are doing it regularly and would not miss a session! One must remember, however, that yoga is very much a process; you never get to the end, because there is always something else to do. Stay with how it feels, inside and out.

I often find that one of the main limitations with yoga is that people think they either have to do an hour and a half a day, or nothing at all. What I am trying to avoid is being the thing on somebody's list that at the end of the day "didn't get done"—and the cause of guilt or regret. I therefore encourage people to start small—three minutes a day, five days a week—thus allowing for a couple of busy or forgetful days. You can do it anywhere: stretch your arms overhead at your desk or sit in your car, close your eyes, and breathe. I am certain that if people committed to three minutes a day, five days a week, they would soon start to feel better and automatically strive to do more.

I strongly believe that if everyone on the planet learned how to breathe diaphragmatically, we would see fewer illnesses, depression, and *bombings*. We would be kinder to ourselves and to everyone else. It is never too late to start!

—Amber Valentyne

You can learn more about Amber Valentyne at: www.ambervalentyne.com

Yanka Van der Kolk—Photographer, Image Artist, Consultant, and Performance Coach

Photo: Yanka Van der Kolk

Although our paths crossed several times, Yanka and I did not connect until we finally met through the Women Entrepreneurs of Canada organization. Since then, we have come together for various purposes, such as participating in meditation circles, working on my portraits, and on this book.

Working with Yanka is an experience in and of itself. Yanka is remarkably talented and insightful in her creation—interacting with her clients in a way that brings out the best in them. Unlike other photographers, Yanka does not focus solely on the final product, but rather on the joy involved in the process.

Before I met Yanka and her husband Henk, I disliked having my photo taken. I was timid and apprehensive about smiling. Working with the two, however, changed me entirely! Through Yanka, I discovered how to open up and truly love my image. She taught me how to use her as my mirror and experience myself through her.

This transformation has been a crucial element in my healing process. Since then, I enjoy showing off my smile and displaying my emotions in photographs, instead of hiding away. I appreciate how much younger, livelier, and more delightful I look when I smile, not only in photos but in my daily life as well.

I believe Yanka's contribution is crucial for the healing of women. She enables women to feel and experience their true selves, embrace their inner and outer beauty, and reveal and stay connected to who they really are.

—Pirjo Friedman

They say that a picture is worth a thousand words; but I believe that in today's society it is worth millions! The power of photography can be illustrated, for example, by the Elvis and Marilyn Monroe industries that would simply not exist without it. Photography produces an eternal image that never changes. It may fade over time, but once it is created, it is what it is. Photos allow us to look back into our past, confirm our knowledge, and revive images and ideas. Without them, our entire past could be questioned, leaving us with no perfect memories, and merely with the question: "*Did we really happen?*"

I grew up as a second child in a strict Calvinist home, and for many years I continuously tried to find my place and discover who I was. Whenever I questioned my parents about their beliefs, they would say, "Who are you to question the Almighty? Do not question these things. Simply believe it." But I could not believe something that I could not imagine.

Growing up, I was taught that as human beings we are in this world, but not of this world. I was too young to grasp the philosophy behind the belief; after all, if I could see myself in photographs, how could I not be a part of this world? I tried to answer this question by examining myself in front of the mirror, despite my parents' objections, who claimed that it was vain and ungodly. I was expected to praise the Lord, not my own face. I was taught that putting oneself first and yearning to be the center of your own attention is wrong. But I could not help myself—I was fascinated by my image in the mirror, by the infinity of emotions, faces, and images I was capable of role-playing. In retrospect, this fascination has been the basis for my two careers: modeling and photography.

I met my husband, Henk, when I was nineteen, and before I knew it, we had three kids. Although I thought I was too young to be a full-time wife and a mother, I soon discovered how much I could learn from my children. My kids exposed me to innocence, and helped me reveal the innocence within me. They made me feel alive and forgiving after many years of living with the guilt and confusion that I was taught at home. Being with my children, there was no longer confusion; I was simply one of them. I wished not to be separated from them like I was from my own parents, and for this reason, I never referred to them as children, but called them Roland, Yolanda, and Lance, and encouraged them to call me Yanka rather than Mother. Living with Henk and my children, I experienced being loved and being the center of attention for the first time, and learned that showing appreciation to ourselves is the first step of learning to love ourselves.

After several years of raising my family, I felt it was time to find a part-time job. I decided to pursue a career in modeling; however, although I convinced myself that auditioning and not getting the job was still a valuable experience, it did not change the fact that no matter how prepared I was for the audition, I never got the job. Once, I came home to my husband, frustrated that I could not become successful and almost ready to give up modeling completely. Henk asked if I believed I could do it, and I replied that I knew I could. He asked why I cared so much about what other people thought of me and expected of me. He advised me to do what I do in a way that I would enjoy the most, and not to make any assumptions about what is right and wrong, or what is anticipated of me. Henk inspired me to create my own ideas and live them. "Who cares if you don't get the job? At least you will have fun trying!" he told me.

Following my husband's advice, we moved into the city, hired a nanny, and freed my schedule so that I could fully prepare myself for the work ahead of me. Several months later Henk finally said, "Today you are going to pick up the telephone and make an appointment for yourself. Who do you wish to call?" I decided to call all the clients that had refused me in the past, starting with a certain large department store.

I phoned, scheduled an appointment, and several days later, I walked through their door, looking my best and full of surface confidence and conviction. I declared that if I did not get the job right then and there, I was never coming back. The girl who auditioned me examined my photographs, smiled, and said, "Well, you are getting better, kid. I would like to use you. Come back in three months once you've got more experience." She was my age, yet she called me "kid."

I stood up tall and crossed my arms. "I am not coming back." I said, "This is your last chance. Give me a break today, and you will have a chance to be the first to discover how great I can be." Although I was in tears by the time

I finished my speech, I managed to impress her. "You have it," she said, "but I am not giving you a break; it was you who just gave yourself one."

That audition led to many years of close work with this company. Although it took another couple of years, it seemed as though I became a top fashion model overnight, working with all the top models of the time. The moment of landing my first job, however, is one that I will never forget! Since then, every time that I witness someone exposing their deep emotions directly from their source, like I did that day, I observe how they are giving themselves a break. And no matter how many times I see it, it always moves me deeply.

Through my career as a model I learned to remain true to myself. As a model, you are the image, the art form. The expressions and personality that you manage to bring out are what create you professionally. This is why it is imperative to be connected and give back to yourself, and not only to others. Throughout my career, I used the mirror role-playing game that I enjoyed as a child. Every time before I appeared in front of a camera, I would confront myself in front of the mirror, and role play, role play, role play! I would try the role on and experiment with it in a hundred different ways. I would conclude by saying to myself, "You are beautiful; that is your gift—appreciate it!" Appreciating my gift of beauty enabled me to love myself without feeling vain. Only after performing this little ritual would I be ready and confident for the job.

My fascination with my current profession began long before my experimentation with modeling. When I was ten years old, my father's employer bought me a Brownie camera, and since then I have been photographing everything in sight: ice on the trees, the sun in a cow's eyes, my own reflection in the mirror. I discovered the miracle of extending my reality—once the sun was down and the ice melted; I still had their photos and the excitement of the moment. I began experimenting with self-portraits, role-playing different attitudes and capturing them on film. Photography became my second mirror, my great love, and later, my career.

When I photograph someone, the process is a play of that person's emotions, physical qualities, and mostly how the person feels about those qualities. Light also plays a role, as well as the eye of the photographer. Anyone who is part of that creation needs to take responsibility for the end result. The photo is created out of true collaboration and the experiencing of each other in true harmony.

I view photography as the art of one's face. It is a powerful idea of yourself—a complete experience of yourself and the sharing of your genuine emotions. Photography allows you to role-play your image—your real feelings and emotions—so that you can experiment and see what they look like, thus achieving greater freedom and flexibility in how you present yourself to the public. Photography allows us to see our emotions ourselves—something we seldom get to see. I believe that celebrities have such a strong connection with the camera because they can actually see into the light—the light of their own imagination. While knowledge is wonderful, imagination is sublime, and it allows for endless creativity. We are attracted to the images of these celebrity actors and models, to the exhibition of their emotions. We are constantly comparing ourselves to these "stars." How can we not be? They are brilliant images!

One of the things I found most fascinating with photography was discovering what makes other people beautiful. I believe it is important for a person to reveal this element, since it reflects on what actually fascinates us about ourselves. Through photography, I could experience and appreciate how and why people have the ability to shine through with their eyes.

Displaying emotions is not only about how other people see you, but rather it is about how you see yourself. Some people tell me I am very confident. Maybe they are, too, but where do I look for it? You must find a way to express your confidence openly. You need to see it when you look into your own eyes. Only then will you have the power to show it to the world. If you cannot see it when you look at yourself, others will not see it either. You might as well put up a sign saying, "Confidence inside" or "It's in my socks." This life-long quest for our own confidence is a living process.

When you wish to feel beautiful and love yourself, you must reach to the source of your self, your soul, which is reflected in your eyes. If your heart is closed, your eyes will appear frozen and blank in the photo. However, an honest connection with the camera will reveal one's inner beauty. A powerful photograph is one where your true self is reflected through your eyes—the "windows of our soul." The camera cannot lie—you can dress up, apply make-up, and make a face, but you will not escape the image of your soul that emerges. That is the miracle of a photograph.

The first few times Pirjo and I met, we did not connect straightaway. Although Pirjo was always friendly, and I am a social person myself, I was slightly intimidated by her eyes, which were cool, somewhat distant and reserved. I could not easily read her and her emotions simply by looking in her eyes. It was not until Pirjo contacted me in one of my seminars and we began to work together on her portraits that she learned to express herself through her eyes and let her inner self shine through.

The search for identity is embedded deep within us. I am convinced that every human being needs to be visible to herself. You do not need to wait for the public to make you visible by gaining success, acceptance, and recognition. In fact, you can begin the process with the privacy of your own mirror. I often teach my clients the mirror role-playing game. I call it "the case before the mirror," and it is as effective as it is simple! All you need to do when you wake up is go to the mirror and look for yourself—for your freedom. When you see your face, greet it and say, "Oh, there you are!" Your schedule for that day is completely irrelevant, whether you are going through your ordinary daily routine or expecting something fresh and exciting to occur, the second you confront your own eyes, you turn on your energy. Tell yourself, "I love who I am. I love my face. I am beautiful. I am excited!" Tell yourself whatever comes to your mind—whatever makes you feel good. Connect with your soul; with whatever you are feeling that morning. If you are not in a particularly happy mood, embrace the "child" in you and inquire, "My dear, what happened? What is the matter?" Use what I like to call "the eyes of love." Look at yourself with the patience of a parent, with trusting eyes of kindness and forgiveness.

Seeing yourself every morning is a powerful tool that teaches you not to be afraid of confronting your emotions. Do not be afraid of being who you are in any situation. Do not be afraid to stand alone. You do not have to be liked in order to be real and relevant. In our society many are trying too hard to be liked. We strive to consume, wear, eat, and look like admired symbols, symbols of power and greatness, symbols of what our society values as a standard for beauty. Our standard for beauty, however, is something that only we can explore through our own experience of ourselves. Trust your passions since they arise from yourself. Once you can do that, you can begin to laugh, shout, show your energy freely, and to use your courage and curiosity. Be the child within you; become yourself. In the mirror you can find harmony with your soul energy once again.

Today's society allows me to pursue my photography career for the rest of my life, as our society is becoming more and more visible, and we can no longer hide from our own self-image. I feel lucky to be a part of a happy business that I love, and that allows me to assist people in seeing how beautiful they are through their own eyes.

—*Yanka Van der Kolk*

You can learn more about Yanka Van der Kolk at: www.yanka.ca